FILMMAKERS SERIES
edited by
ANTHONY SLIDE

1. *James Whale*, by James Curtis. 1982
2. *Cinema Stylists*, by John Belton. 1983
3. *Harry Langdon*, by William Schelly. 1982
4. *William A. Wellman*, by Frank Thompson. 1983
5. *Stanley Donen*, by Joseph Casper. 1983
6. *Brian De Palma*, by Michael Bliss. 1983
7. *J. Stuart Blackton*, by Marian Blackton Trimble. 1985
8. *Martin Scorsese and Michael Cimino*, by Michael Bliss. 1985
9. *Franklin J. Schaffner*, by Erwin Kim. 1985
10. *D. W. Griffith and the Biograph Company*, by Cooper C. Graham et al. 1985
11. *Some Day We'll Laugh: An Autobiography*, by Esther Ralston. 1985
12. *The Memoirs of Alice Guy Blaché*, 2nd ed., translated by Roberta and Simone Blaché. 1996
13. *Leni Riefenstahl and Olympia*, by Cooper C. Graham. 1986
14. *Robert Florey*, by Brian Taves. 1987
15. *Henry King's America*, by Walter Coppedge. 1986
16. *Aldous Huxley and Film*, by Virginia M. Clark. 1987
17. *Five American Cinematographers*, by Scott Eyman. 1987
18. *Cinematographers on the Art and Craft of Cinematography*, by Anna Kate Sterling. 1987
19. *Stars of the Silents*, by Edward Wagenknecht. 1987
20. *Twentieth Century-Fox*, by Aubrey Solomon. 1988
21. *Highlights and Shadows: The Memoirs of a Hollywood Cameraman*, by Charles G. Clarke. 1989
22. *I Went That-a-Way: The Memoirs of a Western Film Director*, by Harry L. Fraser; edited by Wheeler Winston Dixon and Audrey Brown Fraser. 1990
23. *Order in the Universe: The Films of John Carpenter*, by Robert C. Cumbow. 1990 (*out of print; see No. 70*)
24. *The Films of Freddie Francis*, by Wheeler Winston Dixon. 1991
25. *Hollywood Be Thy Name*, by William Bakewell. 1991
26. *The Charm of Evil: The Life and Films of Terence Fisher*, by Wheeler Winston Dixon. 1991

27. *Lionheart in Hollywood: The Autobiography of Henry Wilcoxon*, with Katherine Orrison. 1991
28. *William Desmond Taylor: A Dossier*, by Bruce Long. 1991
29. *The Films of Leni Riefenstahl*, 2nd ed., by David B. Hinton. 1991
30. *Hollywood Holyland: The Filming and Scoring of "The Greatest Story Ever Told,"* by Ken Darby. 1992
31. *The Films of Reginald LeBorg: Interviews, Essays, and Filmography*, by Wheeler Winston Dixon. 1992
32. *Memoirs of a Professional Cad*, by George Sanders, with Tony Thomas. 1992
33. *The Holocaust in French Film*, by André Pierre Colombat. 1993
34. *Robert Goldstein and "The Spirit of '76,"* edited and compiled by Anthony Slide. 1993
35. *Those Were the Days, My Friend: My Life in Hollywood with David O. Selznick and Others*, by Paul Macnamara. 1993
36. *The Creative Producer*, by David Lewis, edited by James Curtis. 1993
37. *Reinventing Reality: The Art and Life of Rouben Mamoulian*, by Mark Spergel. 1993
38. *Malcolm St. Clair: His Films, 1915–1948*, by Ruth Anne Dwyer. 1997
39. *Beyond Hollywood's Grasp: American Filmmakers Abroad, 1914–1945*, by Harry Waldman. 1994
40. *A Steady Digression to a Fixed Point*, by Rose Hobart. 1994
41. *Radical Juxtaposition: The Films of Yvonne Rainer*, by Shelley Green. 1994
42. *Company of Heroes: My Life as an Actor in the John Ford Stock Company*, by Harry Carey Jr. 1994
43. *Strangers in Hollywood: A History of Scandinavian Actors in American Films from 1910 to World War II*, by Hans J. Wollstein. 1994
44. *Charlie Chaplin: Intimate Close-Ups*, by Georgia Hale, edited with an introduction and notes by Heather Kiernan. 1995
45. *The Word Made Flesh: Catholicism and Conflict in the Films of Martin Scorsese*, by Michael Bliss. 1995
46. *W. S. Van Dyke's Journal: White Shadows in the South Seas (1927–1928) and other Van Dyke on Van Dyke*, edited and annotated by Rudy Behlmer. 1996

47. *Music from the House of Hammer: Music in the Hammer Horror Films, 1950–1980*, by Randall D. Larson. 1996
48. *Directing: Learn from the Masters*, by Tay Garnett. 1996
49. *Featured Player: An Oral Autobiography of Mae Clarke*, edited with an introduction by James Curtis. 1996
50. *A Great Lady: A Life of the Screenwriter Sonya Levien*, by Larry Ceplair. 1996
51. *A History of Horrors: The Rise and Fall of the House of Hammer*, by Denis Meikle. 1996
52. *The Films of Michael Powell and the Archers*, by Scott Salwolke. 1997
53. *From Oz to E.T.: Wally Worsley's Half-Century in Hollywood—A Memoir in Collaboration with Sue Dwiggins Worsley*, edited by Charles Ziarko. 1997
54. *Thorold Dickinson and the British Cinema*, by Jeffrey Richards. 1997
55. *The Films of Oliver Stone*, edited by Don Kunz. 1997
56. *Before, In and After Hollywood: The Autobiography of Joseph E. Henabery*, edited by Anthony Slide. 1997
57. *Ravished Armenia and the Story of Aurora Mardiganian*, compiled by Anthony Slide. 1997
58. *Smile When the Raindrops Fall*, by Brian Anthony and Andy Edmonds. 1998
59. *Joseph H. Lewis: Overview, Interview, and Filmography*, by Francis M. Nevins. 1998
60. *September Song: An Intimate Biography of Walter Huston*, by John Weld. 1998
61. *Wife of the Life of the Party*, by Lita Grey Chaplin and Jeffrey Vance. 1998
62. *Down But Not Quite Out in Hollow-weird: A Documentary in Letters of Eric Knight*, by Geoff Gehman. 1998
63. *On Actors and Acting: Essays by Alexander Knox*, edited by Anthony Slide. 1998
64. *Back Lot: Growing Up with the Movies*, by Maurice Rapf. 1999
65. *Mr. Bernds Goes to Hollywood: My Early Life and Career in Sound Recording at Columbia with Frank Capra and Others*, by Edward Bernds. 1999
66. *Hugo Friedhofer: The Best Years of His Life: A Hollywood Master of Music for the Movies*, edited by Linda Danly. 1999

67. *Actors on Red Alert: Career Interviews with Five Actors and Actresses Affected by the Blacklist*, by Anthony Slide. 1999
68. *My Only Great Passion: The Life and Films of Carl Th. Dreyer*, by Jean Drum and Dale D. Drum. 1999
69. *Ready When You Are, Mr. Coppola, Mr. Spielberg, Mr. Crowe*, by Jerry Ziesmer. 1999
70. *Order in the Universe: The Films of John Carpenter*, 2nd ed., by Robert C. Cumbow. 2000
71. *Making Music with Charlie Chaplin*, by Eric James. 2000
72. *An Open Window: The Cinema of Víctor Erice*, edited by Linda C. Ehrlich. 2000
73. *Satyajit Ray: In Search of the Modern*, by Suranjan Ganguly. 2000
74. *Voices from the Set: The* Film Heritage *Interviews*, edited by Tony Macklin and Nick Pici. 2000
75. *Paul Landres: A Director's Stories*, by Francis M. Nevins. 2000
76. *No Film in My Camera*, by Bill Gibson. 2000
77. *Saved from Oblivion: An Autobiography*, by Bernard Vorhaus. 2000
78. *Wolf Man's Maker: Memoir of a Hollywood Writer*, by Curt Siodmak. 2001
79. *An Actor, and a Rare One: Peter Cushing as Sherlock Holmes*, by Tony Earnshaw. 2001
80. *Picture Perfect*, by Herbert L. Strock. 2000
81. *Peter Greenaway's Postmodern/Poststructuralist Cinema*, edited by Paula Willoquet-Maricondi and Mary Alemany Galway. 2001
82. *Member of the Crew*, by Winfrid Kay Thackrey. 2001
83. *Barefoot on Barbed Wire*, by Jimmy Starr. 2001
84. *Henry Hathaway: A Directors Guild of America Oral History*, edited and annotated by Rudy Behlmer. 2001
85. *The Divine Comic: The Cinema of Roberto Benigni*, by Carlo Celli. 2001
86. *With or Without a Song: A Memoir*, by Edward Eliscu. 2001
87. *Stuart Erwin: The Invisible Actor*, by Judy Cornes. 2001
88. *Some Cutting Remarks: Seventy Years a Film Editor*, by Ralph E. Winters. 2001
89. *Confessions of a Hollywood Director*, by Richard L. Bare. 2001
90. *Peckinpah's Women: A Reappraisal of the Portrayal of Women in the Period Westerns of Sam Peckinpah*, by Bill Mesce Jr. 2001

91. *Budd Schulberg: A Bio-Bibliography*, by Nicholas Beck. 2001
92. *Between the Bullets: The Spiritual Cinema of John Woo*, by Michael Bliss. 2002
93. *The Hollywood I Knew: 1916–1988*, by Herbert Coleman. 2002
94. *The Films of Steven Spielberg*, edited by Charles L. P. Silet. 2002
95. *Hitchcock and the Making of Marnie*, by Tony Lee Moral. 2002
96. *White Horse, Black Hat: A Quarter Century on Hollywood's Poverty Row*, by C. Jack Lewis. 2002
97. *Worms in the Winecup: A Memoir*, by John Bright. 2002
98. *Straight from the Horse's Mouth: Ronald Neame, An Autobiography*, by Ronald Neame. 2003
99. *Reach for the Top: The Turbulent Life of Laurence Harvey*, by Anne Sinai. 2003
100. *Jackie Coogan: The World's Boy King: A Biography of Hollywood's Legendary Child Star*, by Diana Serra Cary. 2003
101. *Rungs on a Ladder: Hammer Films Seen through a Soft Gauze*, by Christopher Neame. 2003
102. *The Classically American Comedy of Larry Gelbart*, by Jay Malarcher. 2003
103. *Perpetually Cool: The Many Lives of Anna May Wong (1905–1961)*, by Anthony B. Chan. 2003
104. *Irene Dunne: The First Lady of Hollywood*, by Wes D. Gehring. 2003
105. *Scorsese Up Close: A Study of the Films*, by Ben Nyce. 2003
106. *Hitchcock and Poe: The Legacy of Delight and Terror*, by Dennis R. Perry. 2003
107. *Life Is Beautiful, but Not for Jews*, by Kobi Niv, translated by Jonathan Beyrak Lev. 2003
108. *Young Man in Movieland*, by Jan Read. 2004

Young Man in Movieland

Jan Read

Filmmakers Series, No. 108

The Scarecrow Press, Inc.
Lanham, Maryland, and Oxford
2004

SCARECROW PRESS, INC.

Published in the United States of America
by Scarecrow Press, Inc.
A wholly owned subsidiary of
The Rowman & Littlefield Publishing Group, Inc.
4501 Forbes Boulevard, Suite 200, Lanham, Maryland 20706
www.scarecrowpress.com

PO Box 317
Oxford
OX2 9RU, UK

Copyright © 2004 by Jan Read

Unless otherwise credited, all photographs courtesy of the author.

All rights reserved. No part of this publication may be reproduced, stored in a retrieval system, or transmitted in any form or by any means, electronic, mechanical, photocopying, recording, or otherwise, without the prior permission of the publisher.

British Library Cataloguing in Publication Information Available

Library of Congress Cataloging-in-Publication Data

Read, Jan, 1917–
　Young man in movieland / Jan Reed.
　　p. cm. — (Filmmakers series ; no. 108)
　ISBN 0-8108-4449-4 (alk. paper)
　1. Read, Jan, 1917– 2. Screenwriters—Great Britain—Biography. 3. Screenwriters—United States—Biography. 4. Motion picture industry—United States. 5. Motion picture industry—Great Britain. 6. Television writers—Biography. I. Title. II. Series.
PR6035.E323 Z477 2003
808.2'3'092—dc21

2003011523

∞™ The paper used in this publication meets the minimum requirements of American National Standard for Information Sciences—Permanence of Paper for Printed Library Materials, ANSI/NISO Z39.48-1992.
Manufactured in the United States of America.

To Maite, who shared so much

Contents

	Preface	xiii
Chapter 1	Preview	1
Chapter 2	New York, New York	13
Chapter 3	California, Here I Come	33
Chapter 4	125th Street	45
Chapter 5	Hollywood, Reel 2	57
Chapter 6	The Polish Corridor	67
Chapter 7	Doctors and Patients	95
Chapter 8	At the King's Head and Eight Bells	105
Chapter 9	The Spanish Connection	119
Chapter 10	Monsters and Little Green Men	131
Chapter 11	Where We Came In	141
	Index	151
	About the Author	157

Preface

The immediate postwar period was a fascinating one in the history of movies. They were golden years in a Hollywood as yet unthreatened by television, while in Britain the Rank Organisation, London Films, and Ealing Studios were turning out pictures on a scale and of a quality as never before. Though we were not to know it at the time, this was the last great fling of the film industry.

The book began as an account of three impressionable years from 1946 to 1949, when I was beginning as a movie writer in Hollywood and London, and I have linked together stories and sketches written at the time with a connective narrative putting them in context. The temptation was then to continue, because it seemed worthwhile to leave some record of talks with Dylan Thomas or Boris Karloff, the struggle to shoot a documentary in Venice on the proverbial shoestring, the making of the "Superdynamated" epic *Jason and the Argonauts*, and the inside stories of movies with which I was concerned—some of them blockbusters, some flops, and some (among them my favorite, *The Beach at Falesa*) never made at all.

It is not the easiest thing for a scriptwriter, forever putting words into other people's mouths, to take center stage. The pitfall is to dramatize and justify oneself, but as the great Marcel Pagnol once said, "I shall expose myself entirely by the way I write, and if I am not sincere—that is to say, without any shame—I shall have wasted my time and spoilt good paper."

I am grateful to Carlton International Media, Ltd., for permission to reproduce the extract from Dylan Thomas's *Me and My Bike* in chapter 6; to Professor David Kemp, the Department of Computational Sciences of the University of St. Andrews; and to my son, John Carlos Read—who between them effected the tricky transfer of the manuscript to diskette.

CHAPTER ONE

Preview

If the documentary was not a British invention, it was the films of John Grierson, Paul Rotha, Basil Wright, Pat Jackson, Edgar Anstey, and the others that made it a household word in the 1930s. Their mantle has long descended on the BBC and various television companies, and though the battle to show documentary films in theaters was fought and lost, they are now shown on television in a variety and on a scale undreamed of by those founding fathers of the movement. When I made up my mind in my late teens to work in movies, it was on the strength of a passionate interest in photography, undying devotion to Katharine Hepburn and Greta Garbo, and regular visits to the "flicks," whether an Astaire-Rogers musical or, as I grew more sophisticated, Fritz Lang's *Metropolis* or the rarely shown foreign films of René Clair or Marcel Pagnol. It was, however, on fashionable documentary that I set my sights. Coming as I did of an academic father and mother, who regarded the antics of the commercial film industry with little less than horror, I also realized that I was much likelier to gain their grudging support for a career—if the word could be applied to such a raggle-taggle activity—in documentary than in the maelstrom of entertainment films.

This was decades before courses in media studies became available from every British university, before a time when film academies and scriptwriting courses offer instant access to filmmaking and their alumni are paid large sums from the government and National Lottery to make films that are never seen in a theater. In short, filmmaking has become respectable in a way that it was not when I set out to storm Hollywood. When I look back it astonishes me to think quite how wide the gulf was between life in the quiet Scots town where I was brought up and the career I had cut out for myself. St. Andrews is best known as the home of golf and for its university, the oldest in Scotland. When my father arrived in the early 1920s to become professor of chemistry, the town was very much geared to the convenience of the university and of a well-to-do retired community, largely Anglo-Indian. Former generals, colonels, and colonial administrators settled there to occupy their days on the golf courses and at the Royal and Ancient Club, and to educate their sons and daughters. Despite its small size the town had its own power station (supplying, of course, direct current) and its gas works. There were lampposts in the streets, attended by a lamplighter, who proceeded with measured pace from one to another with a hooked pole, turning on the lamps and leaving a jeweled train in his wake. There was still a flourishing fishing community, with broad-beamed, brightly colored boats that put out into the bay for their catches of whitefish and herring. A thriving industry turned out hickory shafts and heads for golf clubs, and the city possessed its own brewery—the malting kilns dominated the main street.

Life in that northern outpost was in fact nearer to Jane Austen than it was to today. Entertaining, for example, was a great deal more elaborate than it is nowadays. Dinner ran to many courses, served by a maid in white gloves, with the wines in proper rotation. Evening dress was obligatory for *any* evening function, as were tails for dances. The Anglo-Indian community wore evening dress for dinner every night, whether there were guests or not, except on Sundays, when lounge suits were the form. Part of the enjoyment of an evening party was the arrival of the horse-drawn "growler," with its flickering oil lamps, its intimate interior smelling of worn, quilted leather, and its weather-beaten, ruddy-complexioned coachman in brushed-up top hat (this remained the standard form of transport in St. Andrews until the outbreak of World War II).

From an early age my brother and I were entrusted to a nanny, the daughter of a former Open Champion, who arrived just after lunch (thus leaving my mother free for afternoon bridge parties) and marched us down to the duffers' course to be instructed in the rudiments of golf. Later, one's days were spent at a preparatory school, appropriately enough conducted by the stern Mr. Lemaitre, whose extraordinary achievements in schooling his pupils in the composition of Latin hexameters and the gaining of open scholarships were recorded in covies of wooden shields, lining the walls and gently clattering in the breezes of the largely unheated classrooms. My main release from this well-regulated existence was in visits to the local cinema, where I spent my shilling and became an addict of Charlie Chaplin and Buster Keaton, and of such silent films as *Metropolis*, *The Flag Lieutenant*, *Wings*, and those serials in which the heroine was left strapped to the railway track in the face of an advancing train. Later, when I went to boarding school and university, these glimpses of a world beyond St. Andrews and its golf courses were extended by the opening of the Abbey Bookshop. Picturesquely accommodated in the arched entrance of a medieval house, it specialized in art books, limited editions, avant-garde literature, and elegant pornography (carefully locked away), and it was run by an intellectual who, though of Polish origin, edited the nationalistic *Modern Scot* and departed abruptly at the outbreak of war to open a similar establishment in Washington.

It was a shared enthusiasm for cinema and painting (discovered at the unlikely venue of the badminton club) that resulted in a love affair that was to last for ten years of my life and lead to me to pursue my dream of working in films, and Yvonne to go to the Slade School and become a painter. We were oddly paired. She was the orphan granddaughter of a cattle magnate with ranches in Mexico and Australia; she lived with her sister and authoritarian grandmother in a Scots baronial mansion (now a university residence) staffed by a butler, footman, chauffeur, parlor maid, kitchen maid, lady's maid, cook, and scullery maid—not to mention gardeners. Petite, grey-eyed, husky-voiced, lively minded, and a bit dreamy, she did not pay much attention to clothes—though when she dressed up and I took her to a dance (in one of the four-wheelers), I thought her the most wonderful girl ever. We spent as much time together as her watchful guardian would allow. Our pursuits were innocent enough—walking on the sands, talking about books and paintings, going to the cinema, picnicking, and playing tennis (in that age of innocence, sex was out of the question, and we did not become lovers until after she had married and divorced). In the upshot I persuaded her grandmother, who reminded me of no one so much as Lady de Bourgh in *Pride and Prejudice*, that Yvonne should be allowed to study painting at the Slade School—which for the time being was my undoing, since she married a fellow student, a psychotic South African who in due course set on her with a knife.

As for me, my dream of working in films remained a dream. There was no recognized way of entering the industry, especially from St. Andrews, where I might as well have been on the moon. I therefore went to university, following in my father's footsteps by taking chemistry. There was, however, an interlude. My photographic skills came to the notice of the authorities of St. Leonards School, a large, long-established boarding school for girls in St. Andrews. It was about to celebrate the diamond jubilee of its founding, and I was asked if I would be interested in making a 16 mm film to celebrate it. I jumped at the opportunity, borrowed a sophisticated Zeiss Movikon camera from my friend Oscar Oeser of the university's Psychology Department, and enlisted his services with it. Oscar was one of a small, free-thinking coterie that included Edwin Muir, the writer, and was no supporter of private education. He took part, I think, out of curiosity but joined in with a will and offered me the run of his department's small cutting room. I spent most of my first summer vacation from Cambridge in making a forty-five-minute silent film about life at the school. (A year or two ago I discovered to my surprise that it is now part of the Scottish National Film Archive.) I regarded the prospect of returning to Cambridge with dismay. The year that I spent there was one of the loneliest and unhappiest of my life. I was marooned in uncomfortable digs, had no friends, and found few interests in common with my fellow science students. My sojourn was relieved only by joining the Arts Society, where I met W. H. Auden, and writing reviews of plays at the Arts Theatre for *Varsity Weekly*.

My father, who had been a don at Cambridge and had many friends there, including Canon Raven, the master of Christs, with whose daughter, the charming Peggy, I spent the occasional pleasant afternoon punting on the river, was no doubt disappointed by my negative reaction to the place. However, he was a wise and understanding person, and fellow of the Royal Society and illustrious scientist though he was, his interests went far beyond chemistry. He was an authority on alchemy and a leading scientific historian, and as a young man in his native Somerset had published short stories and written plays in dialect, forming a touring company, the Mendip Players, to perform them. These had come to the notice of Thomas Hardy, with whom he became firm friends. (Much later, on a family holiday in Dorset after Hardy's death, I remember visiting Max Gate and meeting his second wife.) My father evidently had a good deal of sympathy with me, and without saying anything went to some lengths to get in touch with Paul Rotha, a leading exponent of documentary film.

So it was that one day in the early summer of 1937 I found myself in the somewhat decrepit office of the famous Rotha in London's Soho Square. He was a short, thickset man with a balding head and the trace of a cockney accent, and he was sympathetic, if discouraging. "What have you done?" he asked. I explained that I was a keen photographer and that I had written some short stories and poems. He shook his head and said, "Go and get *any* experience and come back in a few years." He added, registering my disappointment, "If you are interested in documentary, a degree in economics would help." Economics and sociology were then the preoccupations of British documentary filmmakers, headed by John Grierson, but Rotha himself had gone to the Slade School and been a painter before entering films. Despite his discouraging words, he was a kindly man, and my excitement knew no bounds when a month or two later I received a telegram offering me the job of assistant, or general dog's body, at twenty-five shillings a week on a small documentary that he was making for the Great Western Railway in Cornwall.

My instant response was to take the first train to Truro. Rotha made no appearance, and the job of shooting the film was left to the director Jack Pollard, cameraman Jo Jago, and myself. Jo, who coupled every adjective with either "fucking" or "buggering," was a native-born Cornishman of Spanish descent from Mousehole. As there was no script—or not at least until one wet day when we sat down in a hotel in Truro to make one up—we filmed wherever he drove us: to the china clay dumps, sparkling in the sun like miniature Alps; the tin mines; or the rocky coast. Our equipment was of the simplest, the main item being a rugged, clockwork-driven Newman-Sinclair camera, in the shape of a large and immensely heavy aluminium box, used generally for location filming at the time. Since it would take only two hundred feet of 35 mm film at a loading, the custom was to buy "studio ends," the leftovers from the thousand-foot rolls of film used in the more sophisticated studio cameras. There was no sound recording equipment; even the expensively budgeted FitzPatrick *Traveltalks* and Fox *Magic Carpet* series were shot mute, and the commentary was added later. Jo did not use an exposure meter but surveyed the scene through a view finder with a dark glass ("fucking marvellous") and adjusted his camera accordingly. Each evening we would dispatch the cans of exposed film by rail to a laboratory in Wardour Street and a day or two later would prevail upon the manager of the local picture palace to run the "rushes" after the last house. The Cornish summer passed happily away, at least until, perhaps from excessive exposure to the cliff top breezes, I went down to a chest infection and was reluctantly abandoned in a hotel room while the other two departed for London. I rejoined them briefly in a Dean Street cutting room, but my twenty-five shillings a week was proving too much for the slender finances of the Strand Film company.

By this point term had long since begun at Cambridge, but I resolutely refused to return, and my father, having broad-mindedly allowed me my fling, arranged for me to resume my chemistry course at St. Andrews University. I worked conscientiously and—having, no doubt, inherited some of his talent—eventually graduated with honors. Though the months with Rotha should have taught me how precarious life was in documentary, I was nevertheless still set on joining the film industry, and I am afraid that during those years at St. Andrews I must have seemed moody and unreasonable to my long-suffering parents. Making the best of things, I helped, with Oscar Oeser, to organize a university film society, and on Sunday afternoons we ran at one of the local cinemas foreign films that were otherwise to be seen only at the Academy Cinema and the Curzon in London.

Another unexpected opportunity cropped up. The university had been left a large collection of calotype and wet-plate photographs dating from the 1830s, the work of David Octavius Hill, Thomas Roger, Lawrence Swan Thomson, and other Scottish pioneers. They were in a confused and higgledy-piggledy state in battered albums or stuck to sheets of yellowing paper, and some of them were fading. The principal of the university, Sir James Irvine, knowing of my preoccupation with photography, called me in to take them in hand and to arrange and catalog them. It turned out to be a fascinating job, the collection covering as it did politicians like Sir Hugh Lyon Playfair, university worthies and their families, Tom Morris and other golfing celebrities, genre studies of the fishing community, and street scenes in Edinburgh and St. Andrews. Sir James, however, was evidently pleased with my efforts, since shortly afterward he offered to support me in an application for a Commonwealth Fund Fellowship.

The fund was an organization devoted to sending young graduates from British universities to study in the United States. Movies were at that time rather beyond its ken—the only person to have done anything remotely similar was Alistair Cooke, who had by now started his *Letter from America*—but Sir James was as shrewd as they come and with his puckish smile commented that documentary was the up-and-coming thing and bade me stress its educational aspects. I found that there was a professor at the University of Minnesota who actually ran a small department dedicated to the subject. Invoking the charismatic name of Paul Rotha and, I am afraid, building up my tiny role at Strand Films, I put in my application. To my astonishment I was awarded a fellowship; it was arranged that I was to sail for America on September 1, 1939. Once again the fates were against me; World War II broke out on that same day.

Some half-dozen years and Second World War later, I was measuring the thermal conductivity of TNT in a laboratory at Birmingham University. I had, I might explain, spent the war as a "boffin," first devising ways and means of rendering camouflage fabric invisible to the prying infrared cameras of Nazi spotter planes, and later working on the knotty problem of "stretching" supplies of high explosive in the face of the sinkings in the North Atlantic of munitions ships from America. The years with TNT had not been without excitement, as on one occasion when a glass tube containing some pounds of molten amatol had caught fire in the laboratory, mercifully to be doused with a small Pyrene extinguisher. Nevertheless, my investigations into aberrations of its conductivity around the melting point, which held out a clue as to its explosive properties, began to seem increasingly less relevant with the end of the war. So it was that when a cable was delivered to my bench asking whether I wished to take up my fellowship and spend a year in the United States studying cinematography, my decision was therefore as rapid as it had been to quit Cambridge. Taking off my white laboratory jacket, I set off for the office of the illustrious Sir Norman Haworth, FRS, to ask for his permission to resign and leave for Hollywood. Urbane man of the world that he was, he took it as the most natural of requests, simply saying that he was extremely sorry to lose me and asking when I was to sail.

I had in fact to admit to myself that, interested as I was in documentary, what really enamored me was Hollywood itself. Documentary had always been the Cinderella of the industry, and I still remember the impression made on me by the irruption, as if from another world, into Strand Film's Dean Street cutting room of a lordly young man from Columbia British, clad incongruously for August in an expensive fur coat and in search of stock footage. Columbia British, or even Gainsborough or Gaumont British, were of course very small beer in comparison with the Hollywood studios, but by the mid-1940s Alexander Korda (with films such as *The Private Life of Henry VIII*, made as early as 1933) and J. Arthur Rank (with the Laurence Olivier Shakespeare films) seemed at long last to be putting the British industry on its feet. It was to J. Arthur Rank, who after all had built up his empire from a modest interest in religious films, that I turned for help, in the form of letters of introduction to the American giants. In the meantime I had managed to persuade the Commonwealth Fund that the only practical way of studying American film production was with the film companies themselves. Fortunately for me, a new breed of film was proving very successful in the United States—the "semidocumentary," essentially a story film but based on fact and shot, like *The House on 92nd Street*, entirely on location. When finally I reached the United States and contrived to attach myself to 20th Century–Fox instead of the University of Minnesota, I was therefore able to convince my sponsors that my field was "semidocumentary" and not the Betty Grable musicals for which that most showmanlike of studios was better known.

The war years in Lancaster, at an outstation of the Royal Arsenal in Sheffield and at Birmingham University, had not passed without distractions. With my flame Yvonne happily married, as I thought, I was much attracted to a girl whose family owned a large-type foundry in Sheffield. She was pretty as paint, and I took her on occasion to the blacked-out Grand Hotel, still putting on dinner dances at the height of the blitz that had destroyed half of the city; there we danced to strains of "A Girl in Calico." Again, there was the charming and intellectual daughter of an Oxford professor—how and where I met her in wartime Britain I cannot remember—to whom I was briefly engaged before realizing that it would not work out and shamefacedly calling things off.

Then out of the blue I had news that Yvonne was divorced after a murderous attack by the South African painter she had so precipitately married and was in Australia, at one of her grandfather's cattle stations. We began writing to each other, and after a time she returned to England and found herself a job as an animator at the cartoon film project that Mr. Rank, at the height of his empire building, had started in Maidenhead as a counterblast to Walt Disney. I would meet her in London from time to time when up for meetings at the Ministry of Defence and would return to write poetry (my knowledgeable friend Lady Brown later told me that all serious writers begin by writing love poems but never marry the girls they write about).

In the Park
Sitting at the small iron table,
You undo your coat, remove
Your scarf, and then,
Running hand through hair,
You look at me and laugh.
"Is this the tea? Will you pour it?"
But there is no tea (how well you pour).
I sit large and serious and opposite;
You encourage me to talk,
In your eyes a tenderness
Like changing sunlit hills,
Living, dying.
I wonder, falter, stop.
"Oh, no," you say, "I'm not, I'm cold.
You understand that underneath
I'm very cold."

Chapter One

By now I was working in Birmingham and as a respite from that unlovely city used at intervals to spend weekends at Ludlow, on the Welsh Marches. I had begun experimenting with oil painting; in wartime Lancaster I rented an empty photographer's studio and, having blacked it out, would try my hand at still life after a day in the lab. Ludlow, with its magnificent castle and views over the Teme, was the ideal venue for a Sunday afternoon painter—and the warmest tribute I ever received was from a young lad who, when I had set up by the cliff overlooking the river, narrowly inspected my canvas and said, "If you take that to W. H. Smith in Broad Street, they'll give you ten and sixpence for it."

Be that as it may, I invited Yvonne to spend a few days at the Feathers Hotel. It was the first time we had been alone together for any considerable amount of time, and for once reality was better than expectation. We did nothing much but explore the town and castle and walk along the Teme Valley and over the fields to Leintwardine, and it was all as natural as breathing—though she demurred at doing what I was now yearning for. However, a week or so later she rang me and proposed meeting in London for just that. I was hopelessly inexperienced in affairs of this sort and booked a room at the Monico Hotel near Piccadilly Circus, which I regarded as suitably raffish. We duly met and, nervously on my part, registered as man and wife; she took it all with high spirits and once in our room undressed, donned my hat, and laughed at me. I guess she realized that I had never made love before and that, above all with her, was keyed up to a degree.

We saw each other whenever we could that summer before I left for America and made love whenever we did—on her houseboat moored in a reach of the Thames near Maidenhead, where we stripped and bathed. The water was icy, and as we clung to each other afterward she confessed that, shy as I then was, it had been an excuse to get my clothes off. Having been close friends for so long and finally discovered sex together, the urge became so strong that on a walk in the country we would lie together. A day or two before sailing I went to see her in the Highlands, where she was staying with friends. She made her excuses, and we wandered off onto a Scottish hillside, where, it being the last time, we lay in the heather and made love until it grew dark. Of course, I desperately wanted to marry her and hardly needed to tell her so—but circumstances were against us. Brought up as I was, one did not marry a girl without the means to support her, and I had just turned my back on a steady career and was about to launch out afresh on the wide-open uncertainties of movies. All I could do was to write from Hollywood and hope that she would wait for the year that I was away.

Having well and truly burned my boats as a budding scientist, I boarded ship at Tilbury docks in late August 1946—there were then no transatlantic flights, and for long after the end of the war accommodation on passenger liners was booked six months ahead. The *William S. MacLennan* was a rusting Liberty ship of some ten thousand tons, built in the United States in sections later welded together. Having survived years of Atlantic convoys, she was on her way home in ballast to be scrapped. Thanks to a missing propeller blade and a cracked main shaft, her maximum speed was nine knots; she was skippered by a half-caste Mexican and crewed mainly by hot-blooded Puerto Ricans given to knifing one another; as I and her other half-dozen passengers soon discovered, the purser had sold most of the bed linen and provisions on the black market in France. We settled down to a diet of canned grapefruit juice and salt pork, spending the days, soon to turn into weeks, sunbathing in the dismantled gun turrets or losing money to the ship's officers at stud poker. We neared New York, only to be informed of a longshoremen's strike, and headed into a South Atlantic storm, bound for the Gulf of Mexico and Mobile. The seaweed in the heaving blue Sargasso Sea, tangling with the old lady's broken propeller, did nothing to increase her speed.

Within hailing distance of Mobile there was another radio message announcing that the strike was over and that we were to proceed back to New York. This we did, with fine views of Miami, Savannah, and the eastern seaboard, and some three weeks after leaving Tilbury docked in New York. The longshoremen's strike was still in full swing, and it was only by bribing the crew to lend us lengths of rope that we passengers were able to lower our luggage over the side and onto the quay.

CHAPTER TWO

New York, New York

For an Englishman, inured for years to food rationing, clothes coupons, and the shabbiness of a blacked-out and boarded-up London, and more recently to the grapefruit juice and salt pork of the *William S. McLennan*, New York seemed scarcely credible. The skyscrapers blazed with light; the stores overflowed with expensive clothes; you could order what you liked in a restaurant—and, above all, do what you damned well liked at any hour of the day or night.

It was overpoweringly hot and humid when I arrived, in the way that only large cities on the sea like New York and Barcelona can be. I had to change my shirt every time I left my air-conditioned room. Between the heat and the feeling of disorientation, I found it difficult to plan a campaign for storming the bastions of the monolithic American motion picture industry; as it turned out, it proved almost unbelievably easy.

Rank's men in London had given me a letter to Col. Justin ("Jock") Lawrence, the organization's American representative. One of the most brilliant publicists in the United States, Jock had joined the Rank Organisation to negotiate the exhibition of its films in America in return for showing the product of its partners, 20th Century–Fox and Universal Pictures, in the hundreds of Odeon and Gaumont cinemas in the

United Kingdom. It was a somewhat one-sided arrangement, since the Hollywood pictures occupied most of the playing time in British cinemas, whereas *Henry V, Brief Encounter, Odd Man Out,* and the other excellent Rank pictures were little shown in the United States, except in small art houses (the reason always given was that the great American public could not understand English accents). Understandably, the movie moguls in New York and on the West Coast put great store on their relations with Rank—and there was always the lurking suspicion that British films were on the threshold of greater things, so that any emissary of the Rank Organisation—which, with a recommendation from Colonel Lawrence, I was seen to be—was to be handled with care. All this, of course, I only came to understand with time.

I duly went to call on him at his house in Park Avenue and found him at his desk, in shirt sleeves, as was his custom, and wearing a pair of brilliant red braces. Jock, a power behind the scenes in the American movie industry, was a Yale man who, instead of a staid career in banking or the law, had, as he told me when I knew him better, opted for "the road of excitement" as a Hearst reporter. While with the *Los Angeles Examiner* he was the only newspaperman ever to obtain an interview with Greta Garbo. Instructed to get her reaction to a telegram announcing the elopement of her costar John Gilbert with the actress Ina Claire, he mingled with the crew on location and contrived to show her the message, to which her response was, "That feelthy son of a beech!" On the edict of William Randolf Hearst, the scoop was never printed, because of intervention by his mistress Marion Davies at the behest of M-G-M, to whom she was under contract.

Jock was much involved with the Marx Brothers and later, while assistant to David O. Selznick at RKO, was also deputed to look after a lively and rebellious Katharine Hepburn, when she first irrupted on Hollywood, shunning the press and fashionable restaurants and habitually wearing slacks—unheard of for women at the time, thereby starting a vogue for them.

As the public-relations man and later second in command to Sam Goldwyn and with the collusion of Fred Astaire, David Niven, the Marx Brothers, and others, he invented many of the famous Goldwynisms, such as "I just had a great idea—but I don't like it." A wonderful publicity stunt, this was an activity that he studiously concealed from Goldwyn himself, who, though he started life as a glove salesman, became a leading producer of prestige pictures in Hollywood and was sensitive on the subject of the alleged malapropisms. Much later, when Goldwyn was invited to Oxford by the chancellor of the university, Jock made amends with a variation on the original "Include me out" (an invention of songwriter Howard Dietz) by getting him to say, "For years I have been known for saying 'include me out,' but today I am giving it up forever. From now on let me say 'Oxford and Balliol, include me in.'" With this new twist Goldwyn felt free to make fun of the gags and use them to his own advantage.

Jock's career took a more serious direction with the onset of World War II, when he was chosen by the Motion Picture Association of America to head a committee for countering the activities of the German-American Bund and its efforts to induce Hollywood to take a pro-Nazi line. In this capacity he was backed by President Roosevelt and the White House. Still later, with the United States now at war, he became PR for General Eisenhower and a key figure at SHAEF (Supreme Headquarters Allied Expeditionary Force).

Jock Lawrence was a man of vision and broad interests. Wisecracking, direct, brimming with energy, yet warm and sympathetic, he at once entered into the spirit of what I was attempting and asked what he could do to help. I told him hesitantly of my interest in semidocumentary and films like *House on 92nd Street* and *13 Rue Madeleine*.

Without wasting time, he said, "Then you must see Spyros Skouras." And picking up the phone, he arranged an interview with the president of 20th Century–Fox that same morning.

Skouras, who ran the financial affairs of Fox in New York while Darryl Zanuck made the pictures in Hollywood, had had a career as colorful as any of the moguls of the period (many of whom had moved into the movie industry after humble beginnings in amusement arcades or the rag trade); he had begun life as a shepherd boy in his native Greece. I found him in his large and gloomy office on the West Side, a stocky, rather round man in a dark suit, seated at a desk on a low dais with stained-glass windows behind.

He began with cordial inquiries about his friend Arthur (whom, of course, I had never met). I then proffered my letter of introduction from Mr. J. Arthur Rank. He read it briefly, then looked up and said,

"Which of my producers do you want to work with?" I began my piece about semidocumentary and said that I had particularly admired Louis de Rochemont's *House on 92nd Street.* "That's easy," he said. "Louis's shooting a picture right here in New York," and taking the phone, "Have Mr. de Rochemont step in."

I waited, and a burly, serious-looking, red-faced man with rumpled fair hair came in—Louis always looked more like one of the New England farmers from whom he was descended than a film producer. "Hiyah, Spyros," he said in his deep, drawling voice.

Mr. Skouras asked how shooting was going on *Boomerang!*, introduced us, handed over Mr. Rank's letter, and said that he would appreciate it if Louis could use me as an assistant on the picture, then rose and shook hands with me and asked if we would excuse him, as he had a full schedule.

It was fortunate for me that, of all the producers in America, I had wished myself on Louis de Rochemont, who, with his stable New England background, his sense of fair dealing, and his determination to make only pictures in which he believed, was about as far removed from a volatile Hollywood showman as he possibly could have been. He had, as he later told me, made his first movie camera with his own hands, and his interest in films was first in factual reportage and later in dramatizing stories from life, shooting on location where the events had actually taken place and using actors only for the leading roles. In 1934 he persuaded Time-Life, Inc., to embark on *The March of Time*, an entirely new departure that brought journalism to the cinema screen and was the forerunner of the in-depth television reporting of today. The films were distributed by 20th Century–Fox, and when de Rochemont ceased to be involved in their production in 1943, he joined Fox as a regular producer. He had served as a line officer in the U.S. Navy from 1917 to 1923, and his first feature picture for the studio was the dramatized documentary about an aircraft carrier, *The Fighting Lady.*

Louis was a friend of J. Edgar Hoover and was fascinated by espionage—hence his next two successes, *The House on 92nd Street* and *13 Rue Madeleine,* both (if at times tenuously) based on files from the FBI. He could at times be thoroughly neurotic and suspicious, and I remember an arrival at the Town House Hotel in Los Angeles when he insisted on searching the room for hidden microphones. His interest in spies lasted all his life, and I was working for him on the script of a picture about the German underground in World War II shortly before he died.

After that first meeting with Spyros Skouras, he sat down with me, discovered that I knew Edgar Anstey, with whom he had made films in Europe, and evidently decided that I was genuinely interested in what he was doing. With typical generosity and practicality he questioned me about my slender allowance from the Commonwealth Fund, then marched me into the office of Joe Moskiewicz, treasurer of 20th Century–Fox, and extracted from him weekly expenses of fifty dollars—a fortune, compared with the twenty-five shillings from Strand! The preliminaries settled, he asked me with his usual courtesy whether I was free for lunch and hailed a taxi for the Waldorf Astoria, where he had settled for the duration of shooting. We were joined by his wife. Louis did nothing without consulting her, and though I was later treated as a member of the family after spending Christmas with them in New Hampshire—and as such was on occasion told off by Ginnie, for my own good—I sensed that on this occasion, his wife, cool and elegantly dressed, had reservations about her husband's new acquisition.

Louis had first read the story of *Boomerang!* in *Reader's Digest*. It revolved around a small-town attorney, played by Dana Andrews, who in the face of local prejudice and at the risk of his own career, undertook the defense of a suspected murderer, finally obtaining an acquittal and later becoming attorney general of the United States. It was a true story, deftly scripted by Richard Murphy; as his director Louis chose Elia Kazan, who had just completed *A Tree Grows in Brooklyn* but was at the time better known for his work with the New York Group Theater. Apart from Dana Andrews and Jane Wyatt, Kazan cast the picture from regulars of the Group Theater, including Sam Levene, Lee J. Cobb, Karl Malden, Ed Begley, and Arthur Kennedy, many of whom were later to become stars in their own right. True to his principles, Louis shot most of the picture in Stamford, Connecticut, where the actual events had unfolded; many of the small parts were played by local councillors, barmen, policemen, and others. I was even enrolled by Kazan as one of the jurors.

Within a day or two of my interview, I joined the sixty-strong unit in Stamford, in the main as an observer but for one hectic fortnight standing in for Hugh Lester, the publicity man, who had slipped and dislocated his shoulder.

I Went to Tallahassee

First of all, it was very difficult to fight my way into the courthouse, which had been taken over as a going concern, everything from the policemen to the sheriff's mallet included, for the solid stone building was besieged by teenagers and bobbysoxers.

"Where is he?" they shouted. "Bring him out!" Then in unison, "We want Dana, we want Dana!" A second-story window opened, and there on a balcony, amid redoubled shrieks, stood their hero, immaculately suited, square jawed, and smiling. I have a confused picture of bare legs, tossing black hair, scarlet mufflers, and tongues hanging out. He tossed down a few autographs, and the scraps of paper floated hither and thither as they drifted toward the crowd below, very much as torn-up papers had drifted from the deck of my Liberty ship toward the Atlantic.

When he went in it was possible for my car to nose toward the stone steps of the courthouse, and this caused a diversion. I was immediately surrounded.

"I've seen you in movies, haven't I?"

"What's your name?"

"Do you act? No. Then what are you doing here?"

"You're called Read—then you're Walter Reade."

At once autograph books were flourished, pens were pushed into my hand, and I said lamely, "No, I'm not Walter Reade," and struggling forward, "I'm a technician from England." I felt as I said it that I should not escape so easily. There was a unanimous shout, "What *is* a technician?" A girl with pimply complexion and coarse black hair thrust up against me. "You got a camera. Will you see *him*? Can you take a photograph of *him*? I'll buy the film." I brushed her off, and the doors of the courthouse closed behind me.

Inside the halls of justice the shouting was hushed to a murmur, and the first person I saw was a small, angry, bald-headed man whom I afterward learned to be the judge—the real-life judge. He was expostulating with the business manager that the company had turned his court into a circus, and a noisy one at that. I think he particularly objected to the line of canary-yellow recording and generator trucks flanking the front of the court. They were subsequently withdrawn to a less prominent site in the yard at the back, which made it considerably more difficult for the crew to flirt with the fans. (After all, flirting does help a fella to pass the time more quickly than playing gin rummy all day; a real, live Irishman, even an Irishman who learned his brogue in California, means more to a gal than a hero who never comes out by the front door.)

They were playing gin rummy upstairs, too. I reached the top of the marble staircase, when a lithe individual in a rakishly tilted grey felt hat—I soon learned that he was one of the assistant directors—whispered fiercely in my ear, "They're shooting," and pushed me through a doorway labeled Consultation Room.

A chair had been set on a platform in front of the window, and a makeup man was working on a girl with her back to the door. Along one wall hung a row of dresses, along the other people were sitting in chairs, looking as if they had been sitting for a very long time; but the center of interest was a group playing gin rummy. They did not look much like actors, or at least like English actors, who always look more stagy offstage than on. There was a man with a large, smooth face and powder-grey hair; a very old man sunk in a velvet-trimmed greatcoat, whose throat and chin were joined by a loose tongue of flesh; and a man whose impudent brown eyes seemed strangely familiar. As I looked at him I realized that I did not think he was an actor because I thought he was a detective, and I had seen him on Broadway as a detective the week before. The girl I did not recognize when, the makeup man finished, she turned and came toward me.

"Chocolate box," I said to myself, "and not to be trusted an inch." Her eyes were wide set, her features perfect, and her red hair cunningly tumbled with a Tam o' Shanter perched on top. She wore a brown overcoat, wide across the shoulders and very much drawn in at the waist, and, since her dress was low cut, closing with infinite suggestiveness on her bare throat and chest. Even her gait seemed a little wanton; her legs spread a shade as she walked toward me, looked at me full of curiosity, and finally sat down in one of the chairs opposite.

The game of rummy did not interest her much, so she started another game of her own. "Can someone tell me the name of a famous person?"

"Lincoln, Roosevelt, Molotov," came from different sides.

"No, not out loud," she said. "He's going to guess," and she looked at one of the actors opposite. Then suddenly she turned to me with a look so friendly and disarming that all my suspicions at once melted. "Won't *you* suggest a name?"

She looked at me, her eyes shining, then bent her head so that I could whisper into her ear. The artifices of the makeup man were now very evident: the yellow-tan complexion, the black pencilling over her fair eyebrows, and the mascara thick on her lashes. Only the copper of her hair, burnished by the lamplight from the passage, she owed to no makeup man.

"Winston Churchill," I whispered.

She thought for a moment, and her cheeks dimpled as she smiled. "It's a difficult one, but I can do it," and she beckoned the actor. "I went to Boston and spent two days there, and then I went to Tallahassee, and then to Ohio, where I spent three days—three days, got it? And then to Hollywood."

The actor considered and then he said, "Winston Churchill."

"Marvellous," I said. "How do you do it?"

She smiled and shook her head, then bending toward me, "Give me another."

"Greta Garbo," I said.

The doors of the courtroom swung suddenly open, and there was a clatter of feet in the corridor pursued by the insistent, ringing voice of Elia Kazan. "Hey, take it easy! Don't beat the gun, you're reporters, not wildmen! Now you, *you*, c'm on, act it, act it. Your great big head's in the film! Boy, your face is made of stone this afternoon. Smile, smile! That's better. . . . That's fine. . . . Now look, folks, I want you to share this with your neighbors. Jake, you share it with those two girls. That gentleman in the grey hat there at the back, you share it with her . . ."

The noise rose to a crescendo; there was a sudden crash, and the corridor filled with tossing hats and overcoats.

"C'm on, c'm on, now fight, keep on fighting, keep going. . . . Exit, exit, *Get Out!*" The noise was suddenly and unnaturally hushed, and then the voice: "All right, very good, you're a hotshot group all right!" And another voice, Louis de Rochemont's, deep and rolling: "Don't encourage them too much, boy!" General laughter. "Let's go while the steam's on here!" Everybody in his place, this is a take . . ." Both voices were drowned by the returning extras as they pressed down the lobby; the doors swung to, and all was silent again.

The only other girl in the room was so petite as to be almost doll-like. How old was she? Sixteen, nineteen, twenty-three—I don't know, but she was made up for the part of a young girl and looked, with her bare legs, full bosom, and fanning skirts, for all the world like the woodcut illustrations to *Alice in Wonderland*. You looked into her eyes and they were amazingly clear, like a cat's eyes. As she sat, she stretched her hair between her fingers and trimmed the ends with a pair of nail scissors, listening to all that was said without speaking.

"I took a train to Quebec in Canada, and I stayed there one day," began the redhead. The assistant looked around the door and put his fingers to his lips. "Shh, shh. Too much noise. They're still shooting." She continued in a loud whisper, "I took the train to Quebec in Canada and stayed there one day, then I went to Cleveland for two days, and then to Hollywood, and then to Newton, and then to Miami for one day, and then I went to Tallahassee . . ."

"Oh, shucks, give us a chance!" said the actor.

She laughed and began again, and I turned to her friend. "Do *you* know how it's done?" But Alice only looked at me with her clear cat's eyes and shook her head.

"Greta Garbo," said the actor.

The doors to the courtroom opened again, and the arc lights faded. As the actors came out for a breather, the assistant director reappeared.

"You're all wanted for the next shot."

The girls began to comb their hair and touch up their lips. I went into the courtroom and sat down out of range of camera and next to one of the extras, an old man with a lined face and a high, peaked nose. Unlike the more important film folk, he accepted me at once and talked about himself; he was of Irish descent, though he had never seen Ireland, and when I asked why he didn't go there for a vacation he smiled wryly, and I saw that I had made a mistake.

"Been in show business long?" I asked.

"All my life," he said simply. "I've been in movies since they shot them on open-air stages and in studios with glass roofs. I spent six months in Mexico, and we shot different movies alternate days; that was before the last war. Then I went to New Brunswick . . ."

"Ever been to Tallahassee?" I asked.

"No, why should I?" he said, puzzled, and after a pause, "It's a hard life. The union doesn't call me as often as it used to. It's all a matter of luck. Now look at that girl . . ."

I looked up and saw that the redhead had come in and sat down.

"D'you think she can act? She can do one part to the life, and she's got it in this picture. It's all luck and being able to rise to the occasion when it comes," and, he added gravely, "in the end it always will come." I looked at his greying hair, at the vest he no longer filled out. Perhaps it was a question not of taking chances but of making them.

There was a brusque interruption. "Now look, folks, all those steaks you ate at lunch have made you a little sleepy. I, for one, never ate so well in my life. But you got to be on your toes. You're grateful, see, amazed. . . . Let it build, show your admiration . . . and, and think of him as if he was a relation of *yours, your* son, *your* husband . . ." Kazan turned to Dana Andrews, the object of their admiration, who stood, as before, square jawed, honest, heroic, a revolver pressed to his head in a way that would have caused palpitations among the yelping fans outside.

I looked at the redhead. All the directions seemed to be passing over her, and she sat nonchalantly chewing gum. I was inclined to agree with the Irishman about her dramatic capabilities. Meanwhile, Kazan, abandoning his galvanic manner, went up to each of the principal actors in turn, taking one by the hand, patting another on the back and giving him a few last words of advice, and then, "Let's go, folks," and to the camera operator, "It's all yours, Georgie."

The scene unwound like clockwork until the eloquent, manly voice that went with the square-cut chin was suddenly interrupted, outraged.

"Yeah?" she said. It rang out with all the distilled street-corner insolence of Brooklyn. It was blasphemous. I saw what the Irishman meant. Besides that "Yeah," all she did was to nod once or twice, say an equally contemptuous "No," and flounce out, tossing her coppery head; but the shot was a cameo, all right.

"What are we waiting for?" said Georgie Stoetzel, the camera operator. "Let's make some more pictures."

When finally I disentangled myself from the rush of extras, I found the redhead sitting in the window of the Consultation Room, a pack of cards in her hand. She spread them face upward on the windowsill.

"Look the other way," she said to Alice, then beckoned to the makeup man to choose a card. "Ssh, ssh, not out loud, just point to it; she's going to guess." Then to me, "You tell her when she can turn round."

"Now!" I said, and Alice turned.

"Is it this one?" the redhead asked, pointing to the nine of diamonds.

"No," said Alice.

"Or this? Or this?"

"No."

She pointed to the ace of spades.

"Yes," said Alice.

"Now let's change places," said the redhead. "This time I'm going to guess." Then she got up and stood just in front of and below me. She looked straight into my eyes and smiled, and she looked and looked.

"Now," I said, and she turned away toward the cards.

"Is it this?"

"No," said Alice.

"Or this?"

When Alice finally said "Yes," she at once turned her coppery head and fixed me with the same smilingly intent regard. Was she perhaps just watching to see the cards reflected in my eyes?

"Let's try again," I said. "Look at the floor. Can you still do it?"

She could.

And though to this day I don't know how, I do know why she can go to Hollywood or Broadway, or even to Tallahassee, for that matter. (Cara Williams, who was engaged to Sam Levene at the time, was later featured in a number of 20th Century–Fox pictures and went on to star with Danny Kaye in *The Man from the Diner's Club* and in her own television show.)

Kazan was too absorbed in his picture to spare me much time, other than to clap me on the back at intervals and ask me how I was making out. I can still see him, a slim figure in shirt and slacks, with a head of jet-black curly hair, darting in and out of the set, always alert, watchful, acting each part in turn, praising, blaming, exhorting—but always with a joke, a smile, a friendly word.

A Pig in an Alley

The scene is a three-story wooden house on the outskirts of Stamford. Some half-dozen women lean over the balconies, putting out clothes to dry and discussing the murder case that is the central theme of *Boomerang!* Kazan has drilled them over and over again before ever the camera begins to turn. Now the lights are upon them (and any British unit could learn from the expertise of this Hollywood crew, from their sure and skilful handling of lights and recording equipment under the most difficult conditions, from the clockwork precision with which each man does the right thing at the right moment), and when Tom Dudley, the chief assistant, shouts in his deep, throaty voice, "Rolling down!" these Stamford housewives act and enjoy it. Indeed, it is for all the world like charades, except that mistakes are not allowed.

"Cut!" shouts Kazan. "Honey, you say 'The police couldn't pick up a pig in an alley. A pig in an alley, got it?' All right fellas, shoot!"

The camera turns, the women talk, the clothesline creaks and is duly recorded, everything is perfect until the woman begins: "The police couldn't pick up . . ." And she hesitates and stops.

"Hold it, fellas," says Kazan. "Girls, you relax." Then he turns to the offending woman with perfect patience, as if this was the first take and not the seventh. "Now look, Jenny—what's her proper name? Someone tell me her proper name. Suzette? Nice name. Now look, Suzette, you say 'a pig in an alley, a pig in an alley.'" He smiles at the woman, who is aproned and old enough to be his mother, and then, with more than a touch of Groucho Marx, "Gee, baby, I wish I'd known you forty years ago!"

Everyone laughs, and Kazan says, "All right, everybody ready?" The clapper man steps in. "Action!" And this time the camera turns uninterrupted, the difficult lines are said, and Kazan turns to the cameraman and sound engineer. "All right, Georgie? All right, Don?"

"Cameo, Stoetzel," they reply.

"That's your first print," says Kazan. "Girls, that's swell, now once again . . ."

The crew soon accepted me as part of the landscape and at one time or another came over to talk and to ask about filmmaking in England. I, for my part, began to know them as human beings rather than names on the credit list in a darkened cinema: Reid Kilgore, the rakish first assistant; Norbert Brodine, the maestro of the cameras; Booth "Boots" MacCracken, the all-resourceful unit manager; and Don Flick and Roger Heman of the sound department.

However it was Arthur Kennedy, who played the suspect murderer in *Boomerang!*, that I got to know best. Without quite heading the cast, he had played starring roles in a string of films such as *High Sierra*, *The Glass Menagerie*, *The Window*, and *Rancho Notorious*, but although nominated for five Oscars, he was, I think, too restless and too intelligent to fit into the Hollywood pattern. He was certainly a stimulating companion; we often used to eat together, and he liked having me along when he went to the tailor's to order a few new suits. Of my own wartime English wardrobe, bought with clothing coupons, he was frankly incredulous, regarding it as a century or so out of date. It was Arthur Kennedy's strictures on my overcoat that led to a further insight into the complexities of the apparently serious and sober-minded Louis de Rochemont.

The London Overcoat

It was all the fault of the salesman at Austin Reed. Everybody in England knows that when it is a question of going abroad, Austin Reed are the people for clothes. Many a time I have stopped opposite their window in Regent Street and admired the plaster figures with their healthy, brown faces, their pith hats and shorts, their sweaters and climbing boots. So it was with complete confidence that I asked the salesman for a coat warm enough to withstand the rigors of the New York winter. I confess that, even at the time, I was taken aback by that monstrous, grey-flecked, black garment, fiercely belted at the waist and reaching almost to my ankles. I sank visibly toward the floor as he encased me in it. I believe I even protested a little, but the salesman spoke graphically of the icy winds that whistle down the canyons between the skyscrapers, of subzero temperatures and overheated rooms. It was with memories of Victorian engravings of the "Traveller's Farewell to England" and of Fred Astaire, clad in a somewhat similar garment and singing to Ginger Rogers about "yesterday's cold potatoes," that I clasped the great parcel against my breast and made for Piccadilly Circus.

When Louis de Rochement invited me for Christmas, and en route for Portsmouth, New Hampshire, I parked the car outside a hotel in Providence, Rhode Island, the only item of my luggage that the car thieves did not take was that topcoat. I can well understand that they felt it might weigh them down if it came to a question of taking to their heels. Some days after getting back to New York, I was walking, clad in the London overcoat, by a tailor's window near Grand Central Station, when I saw a roll of cloth that took my fancy and went into the shop with the idea of replacing one of the lost suits. The tailor measured me, and as he was helping me into my coat, he looked at me in some astonishment.

"Is there anything else?" he asked. "Shirts? Ties? A lighter coat? I have some beautiful coats."

I hesitated for a moment, and in that moment I was lost. He even put my name into the coat in block letters. Ten minutes later I was walking up Fifth Avenue in an American topcoat, clasping to my breast a brown paper parcel of quite exceptional size.

It was as if Austin Reed had sold me not only a coat but a talisman of extreme potency, for from the moment I laid aside the London overcoat my luck changed for the worse. I pass over the minor irritation, common to all buyers of new hats and coats, of walking straight into the heaviest deluge of the year, so that afterward the new coat looked as if it had been left in disgust in a coach of the Pennsylvania Railroad and retrieved in a lost-property office by an out-at-the-elbows cab driver. I pass over the fact that the sort of man who is once taken for a sucker by a tailor will always be taken for a sucker by another tailor. Instead, I pass straight to the Men's Bar at the Waldorf Astoria Hotel.

I had come with a message for Louis but was met in the lobby by Bill Colleran, another of his assistants, and we went straight to the bar.

"Louis's on the phone to the coast right now," he said. "He'll call us when he's through."

I realized that if Louis had picked up a phone it would be quite some time before he put it down again, so I hung up my coat on the peg opposite. As it was new, I watched it carefully for the first few minutes with the comfortable feeling of security of the man who sits facing the coat pegs and not with his back to them.

The waiter brought us a bottle of Scotch, marked the level of the contents with a red pencil, and then left us. We talked about Louis as his lieutenants always did, to his extreme irritation if he subsequently heard about it. We must have talked for a long time, because the waiter reappeared with fresh supplies of ice, and eventually the level inside the bottle sank from the red pencil mark to the bottom.

"Jesus!" exclaimed Bill, "I'd better call Louis."

He came back a minute later. "Wanted to know why we weren't up there half an hour ago. Let's go." By this time I had quite forgotten that I had a coat, and the waiter had to stop us and give it to me. I hung it over my arm and we made for the elevator.

There are executives in Hollywood who did not even realize that Louis has a sense of humor. They saw him in his office on the coast, at work in his shirtsleeves, frowning and formidable, or driving down Sunset Boulevard and denouncing the gimcrack houses and the cranks who live in them. I remember sitting over lunch one fine Hollywood day and remarking to his secretary, between mouthfuls of the excellent smoked salmon provided by the studio commissary at 20th Century–Fox, that it was undoubtedly a pity that Darryl Zanuck could not have been present in the apartment at the Waldorf Astoria that evening.

Louis was convalescing after influenza and was sitting up in bed writing telegrams. He handed them to Bill. "Type these out for me, will you? I'm going to get up."

"D'you think you ought to?" I said.

"Why the hell not?" and as he shut the bathroom door, "If you're so concerned about my health, call the doctor."

The door opened again. "Go ahead, call him. He's in the hotel."

I took up the phone, and Louis stood by in his shirt tails as the operator tried to connect me.

"Say that you're from the British delegation to the United Nations and you've just given me a shot of penicillin. Say that you're Sir Spenlow . . . Sir Spenlow what?"

I thought for a moment. "Griffiths," I suggested, and then, as the line was connected, I said: "This is Sir Spenlow Griffiths of the British delegation to the United Nations." There was a gurgle at the other end, partly of astonishment, partly of respect. I went on hurriedly and in my best British voice: "I'm ringing up about my poor friend Louis de Rochemont at the Waldorf Astoria. . . . Yes, he's very ill. I've just given him . . ." I put my hand over the phone. "What did you say I'd given you?" I asked Louis urgently.

"A large shot of penicillin," he whispered.

"A large shot of penicillin, Dr. Jordan," and I added, warming to the game, "I gave him a shot of sulfa, too."

"Penicillin *and* sulfa!" said the doctor in alarm. "What's his temperature?"

I hedged. "Would you like to speak to Mr. de Rochemont?" and, in great relief, handed over the phone to Louis, who was listening with a grin that can only be called seraphic.

"Yeah," he croaked in a barely audible voice, "very bad . . . breathing difficult." Then, in response to the prolonged crackles in the telephone, he said goodbye and hung up. He sat back on the bed looking for all the world like a boy who has successfully raided an orchard. "The doctor's coming right up," he said.

"Coming up?" I echoed aghast.

Louis got off the bed and continued dressing. "Do you want to eat, Jan? Bill, would you like some dinner?"

"But how about the doctor?" I said.

"He'll find us," and, adjusting his tie with one hand, he picked up the telephone with the other. "Operator? Give me the French Room, please." He turned to us, "It'll be crowded, but we'll get a table. . . . Hello? Hello, is that the French Room? This is the Marquis de la Pomme de Terre. . . . Yes, I have two members of the French cabinet with me. . . . Yeah, straight away, the table by the steps."

And that was where Dr. Jordan traced us half an hour later. My appetite was failing when I ordered steak and au gratin potatoes, but when the little man appeared at the entrance, hat and coat in hand, I just put down my knife and fork and tried to cover my confusion over a cup of coffee.

Louis was not in the slightest abashed and gave no reason for the departure from his bed of sickness. "Doctor, I want you to meet Sir Spenlow Griffiths. Of course you know of him as a leading British neurologist and a member of the British Medical Council."

My knowledge of medicine being confined to the printed instructions issued with first-aid boxes, our conversation was a little limited, but the doctor, sipping the brandy that Louis had ordered for him, continued to address me as Sir Spenlow, and my confidence rose as I talked of tannic acid, acriflavin, gauze dressings, and the difficulty of obtaining such commodities in wartime Britain. It was only when we stepped out of the elevator on the fourteenth floor and the others went on to Louis's apartment that he buttonholed me and I recognized the appalling state of my ignorance.

"Exactly how much penicillin"—he fixed me with an eagle eye—"and how much sulfa did you inject, Sir Spenlow?"

"I believe," I said, writhing in discomfort, "that our procedure is a little different in England. The patient's condition was bad, and I administered a large dose."

"You did," said Dr. Jordan throatily. "How much in Oxford units?"

By now we were through the doorway. I looked appealingly at Louis, who gave not the slightest sign of noticing my discomfiture. Bill was looking the other way and blowing his nose to prevent an immediate explosion of laughter. Dr. Jordan, foiled for the moment—I believe he suspected me of professional jealousy over the details of medical treatment—disappeared into the bathroom and pottered with the bottles. Seeing a chance to escape, I looked wildly for my coat and hat.

The coat wasn't there. I flew through the room in my haste. I looked high and low. I even searched among Louis's suits in the closet, but all I could see was Dr. Jordan's coat, neatly folded under his black hat, and another coat much too small for me. The horrid truth struck me just as Dr. Jordan emerged from the bathroom.

"I must have been given the wrong coat in the Men's Bar," I blurted out—but there was not time to think about the loss of a new coat or the gloomy embrace of the London overcoat, to which I was again to be condemned. I was too anxious to escape Dr. Jordan. "Goodbye, doctor, goodbye," I said, bundling past him toward the elevator and freedom.

He stopped me in the doorway. "Mighty strange, Sir Spenlow. I was given the wrong coat in the bar. I only noticed after I left and I haven't been able to return it. But the name inside the coat was not Griffiths, but Read, Jan Read." He looked me between the eyes. "I'm certainly glad to see my own coat again. This one is so big it would almost fit a man of your height, Sir Spenlow."

As shooting on *Boomerang!* drew to a close in November, I spent increasingly more time with Louis de Rochemont in New York. Apart from producing feature films for Fox, Louis privately ran a company called Pictorial Research, Inc., which made documentary and commercial films and was about to begin a film for the E. R. Squibb drug company in New Brunswick. The idea of a research trip to New Brunswick in Canada appealed to me, and venally, I am afraid, I suggested to Louis that with my scientific background I might script it for him. He looked at me quizzically, reading me like a book, but took me up on the offer.

When we set off for New Brunswick with Bill Colleran, I soon realized that our destination was not Canada but an exceptionally unattractive manufacturing town in New Jersey, just across the Hudson River. Bill, who was not much interested in "nuts and bolts" films and later went on to direct *Windjammer* in wide-screen Todd-A.O. for Louis and later transferred to Hollywood and married Lee Remick, backed smartly out of the project. Louis, after an afternoon perambulating the firm's penicillin plant, retired to the Men's Bar at the Waldorf, drawling, "Gee, I got to take the weight off my puppies," so with poetic justice, I was left in undisputed control of the enterprise.

Louis's main preoccupation at this time was the acquisition of a property for his next feature film for 20th Century–Fox. Richard Murphy, who had scripted *Boomerang!*, was a friend of Arthur Miller, and there was talk of making the as yet unproduced *Death of a Salesman*. Louis was more interested in *Spoonhandle*, a novel about a feud between fishing families in his beloved New England. I had other ideas and suggested a film that wove together stories and factual pieces from *The New Yorker* magazine. Louis had his doubts about a "portmanteau" film but gave hesitant assent to my approaching *The New Yorker*. I duly spoke to its formidable editor, Harold Ross, waxing lyrical about articles like the classical piece about fishing for Blue Point oysters (which, of course, was a favorite of Louis's too) and stressing the financial benefits of a tie-up with 20th Century–Fox. Ross was cagey but seized on my last point. *The New Yorker* was not much interested in film publicity, but James Thurber was ill and in need of funds; Ross believed that he had started a play about the magazine, and if Thurber could be involved in the project, he promised to give it serious consideration.

Hardly believing my luck, I located Thurber in a sanatorium in Hot Springs and spoke to him over long distance. He, like Louis, was hesitant but suggested a meeting in New York. This I spent the next few weeks trying to engineer, only to be pipped at the post when Louis developed an alarming penicillin allergy and was confined to his bed in the Waldorf.

A little later, we happened in one evening at Twenty-One, the former speakeasy and a fashionable rendezvous for writers and show people. Louis looked around the semigloom of the crowded basement room, then made a beeline for a table in the corner. It was occupied by a drawn-looking man in dark glasses, his tall woman companion and another stockier man who was talking animatedly to them.

"You've met Jan Read," said Louis.

"No," replied James Thurber, "but I guess he's that exceptionally persistent young Englishman."

Louis introduced me to his wife and to the third member of the trio, another *New Yorker* stalwart, John O'Hara, and ordered large Scotches.

Try as I could, I was unable to bring round the conversation to the subject of the film. Louis became increasingly involved in an argument with John O'Hara, about what I cannot now remember. Tempers rose, and a Scotch or two later both got up abruptly and made for the exit, with myself on their heels.

Twenty-One is down a flight of steps from the sidewalk. As I emerged, I saw that they had come to blows. I ran forward, but not in time to prevent Louis's being knocked cold against the steps. He came round in a minute or two. I flagged down a cab, helped him into it, and leaving urgent instructions with the doorman to summon Dr. Jordan, urged the driver to make all speed for the Waldorf.

That was the end of my *New Yorker* project, and soon afterward Louis commissioned Richard Murphy to begin work on *Spoonhandle*.

I spent that Christmas with the de Rochemonts and their two children, Gingie and "Little" Louis, at Blueberry Bank, an elegant old clapper-board mansion in extensive grounds on the outskirts of Portsmouth, New Hampshire. It was bitingly cold, and we hardly ventured from the house except to exercise their monstrous Bouvier hounds or to go down to the quay, with the steely blue water lapping against it, to bargain with the lobstermen. Life at Blueberry Bank did not begin until midday, with lunch about 5 P.M. and dinner in the early hours.

Like his brother, Richard, also a distinguished filmmaker and a wine connoisseur and Chevalier du Mérite Agricole (the family was of Huguenot origin, and Richard spent much of his time at his house in France), Louis was a gourmet and a considerable chef. The early evening was spent in consulting *Gourmet* magazine for new ways of cooking the lobster bought earlier. I was instructed in the art of making Scotch old-fashioneds—one of the more lasting skills acquired during my Commonwealth Fund Fellowship—and while I saw to the drinks Louis would, on impulse at 2 or 3 A.M., put through a call to some well-known American novelist. He had an uncanny knack of knowing just where and when to reach anyone on whom his attention was focused, focused like a searchlight on a plane or an invisible beam of electrons heating an electrode to incandescence. There were men the length and breadth of the United States who jumped at the sound of a telephone, because they knew that whether they were at a bar drinking, at the drugstore, or just loafing with the neighbor, an imperative voice might start from the phone ordering them to Tucson or Tacoma—and they would go.

The emotional climax of the holiday occurred on Christmas night. Louis had been working in the kitchen all day, stuffing and preparing a huge turkey. We were peacefully sitting in the lounge with our old-fashioneds, when a white-jacketed Louis, hot and perspiring, burst in. He had overheated the oven, and the bird had exploded. He was near tears and, brushing aside all offers of help, barricaded himself in the kitchen to collect his feelings.

CHAPTER THREE

California, Here I Come

Louis de Rochemont hated Hollywood and all its works, but when the holiday ended he began receiving increasingly pressing requests from the coast to report at the studio so as to supervise the editing of *Boomerang!* and to take part in story conferences about *Spoonhandle*.

At that time the movie elite traveled to Los Angeles by train, preferably by the *Santa Fe*. There was snow on the ground in New York, still ablaze with Christmas lights, when I arrived at Grand Central Station with Louis and Ginnie and walked down the red carpet to the streamlined aluminium *Super Chief*. He and Mrs. de Rochemont occupied a large drawing room, while I was allocated a comfortable compartment. There was no need to stir from either during the three-day trip, since the press of a bell would bring an attendant to make the beds or a waiter with drinks or a meal. In fact, apart from a brief appearance during a stopover in Chicago, where it was way below zero, with icicles hanging from the steel pylons of the elevated railway, the de Rochemonts never left their drawing room or changed out of pyjamas and dressing gowns. On the third night the train climbed the Rockies, and next morning dawned cloudless with an azure sky as it began the long descent, passing through orange groves with fruit on the trees as we neared Los Angeles.

It was an abrupt transformation from winter to a morning like the most perfect sunlit day in England, but Louis was in not very good humor as he drove down the long palm-fringed boulevard from Union Station, making a detour for my benefit through Beverly Hills, with its well-watered lawns and lush houses, to point out that they were one and all mock-colonial or straight from the fantasies of *Grimm's Fairy Tales*, and that the people who lived in them were equally gimcrack. He deposited me at a small hotel opposite the Fox lot, where the studio had made me a reservation, and then departed for his hotel, the Town House in downtown Los Angeles, as far removed as possible from the movie scene.

As there was not, for the time being, much for me to occupy myself with, he suggested that I should investigate the work of the different departments of the studio—at the time a huge complex at Fox Hills with a back lot embracing standing sets, such as a railway station complete with trains and a quay with a flotilla of ships at anchor.

I proceeded to look up my old friends from the *Boomerang!* unit— "Boots" MacCracken, Reid Kilgore, Don Flick, and the others—on their home ground and a spent a lot of time on the set of the current Fox epic, *Forever Amber*, a lavish production based on the adventures of Nell Gwynn—at least there can have been no dearth of oranges. My efforts to communicate with its director, Otto Preminger, were somewhat frustrating. It having been pointed out to him who I was, in due course he came over to me, clicked his heels in approved Prussian fashion, and said, "My name is Preminger," then about turned and marched off.

It was also felt that I should be introduced to the star of the film, Linda Darnell.

Meet Miss Darnell

She was sitting at a table with Richard Greene. He had just come from Stage Five, where they had broken for lunch, and sat in buckskin breeches, his long cavalier locks falling over his shoulders, his doublet flung open to bare his manly chest. So that, I thought, must be Linda. She looked as cool as a cucumber. It was a hot day for an Englishman, though I believe a Californian had committed suicide the week before on account of a morning so unaccustomedly cold that the thermometer remained obstinately at eighty degrees. At any rate, I was very hot by the time I had walked past the yellow concrete sound stages and down the main street to the Café de Paris.

She wore a black skirt and snow-white blouse, both perfectly plain and admirably calculated to set off her voluptuous figure. Like all the women who eat in the Café de Paris, script clerks, secretaries, or stars, she was immaculately manicured, stockinged, and shod.

I was really so interested in the menu—six years of wartime England tell on a man—that I was halfway through the salad before I glanced up and saw her looking at me with obvious curiosity. I suppose I *was* an object of interest. I must have been the only man in the Gold Room to be wearing an ordinary suit and a collar and tie. The Gold Room is reserved for directors and the more important actors and writers—and I do not count the tweeds worn by writers as ordinary suits. Besides, they wear their sports shirts open at the neck. I guess my companion and I looked out of place; if we had not been sitting in the Gold Room we should have been put down as extras (period England, 1917), and then, of course, we should have been beneath notice.

My friend was technical adviser on the picture, a lame little man who had left Gloucestershire years ago and had been dozing one afternoon in the Harding Library at UCLA to be woken up and led to a sound stage, where he was paid a lot for giving advice on historical detail, advice that was sometimes neglected in the interests of Art (or so he said with a twinkle in his shrewd, grey eyes).

Well, we passed from onion soup au gratin to crab salad, and then, once again, the waitress flourished the menu, but there is a limit to a wartime English appetite. I eyed the portrait of Darryl F. Zanuck on the opposite wall, wishing that I could face life in the same dynamic fashion, and ordered orange sherbet. Richard Greene got up and went out, but the girl stopped to talk to a group at the next table. Then she sat down, and when I glanced in her direction again—and it was no penance to look that way—I noticed that she was still looking at me. We were finishing our coffee and almost ready to go. I wondered if she would say anything as we went past or whether I ought to. But glances can say so much more than words. They are so impudent, penetrating, and frank. So I said nothing, except to my companion, as we lingered for a moment in the tiled patio, shady with tropical plants.

"And that was Linda Darnell?"

"Who?" he asked.

"Why, the girl opposite us at lunch."

"Heavens, no. She plays bit parts. I believe she's under contract to the studio."

"Thanks," I laughed. "But the black hair and the sultry look?"

"Linda's blonde now. Didn't you know? Nearly all the girls around the studio are blondes. They say the boss admired Connie Bennett and likes girls with fair hair and high cheekbones. As for that little girl, there's a story to her. She fell in love with one of the office messengers, and they were going to be married, but Publicity thought the boy wasn't glamorous enough for a starlet, so they fixed a date for her at Ciro's. One of the young leads. They were married shortly afterward."

"And the messenger boy?"

"He caught the eye of one of the producers, and he's a real star now. But you must meet Miss Darnell. Come along."

I suppose it comes of going to movies. You stare at those pale, moving masks up there on the screen until they become symbols, unrealizable, remote, so that it is difficult to believe that the girl ten feet away across the studio floor, a girl, it may be, of average height, of normal loveliness, the crows feet round her eyes cunningly camouflaged by the makeup man, the girl with the rasping voice, is really the name of your imagination.

Far be it to suggest that any such considerations apply to the lovely Miss Darnell. She looked very beautiful as we watched her from the scaffolding above the set, and she stood with her basket of oranges, caught in the silvery light of the arc lamps. The heavy green camera crane moved noiselessly away from her. The crew, hanging from their cradle, watched her intently as the film spun through the gate from one magazine to the other. When the scene was finished, my friend suggested that I shake hands with her, so we walked across the floor to the corner of the stage where they had installed a trailer for her. He told me to wait, then knocked at the door and went in.

I straightened my tie and smoothed back my hair. In the dim light, it was like waiting at the shrine of a cathedral. I looked at the door of the trailer and heard the noise of voices. My friend came out. "They have one more take, and then she'll see you at the end of the scene." She brushed past us on her way to the set, half-turning to smile as she went by. We sat in the folding canvas chairs at the entrance of the trailer to await her return.

"It's always useful to meet these people," said my friend.

Then there was a ring on the telephone at the stage door.

"Mr. Read, Mr. Jan Read," called the studio policeman. "Telephone for you."

I walked to the door, and there, at the other end, was a deep voice. "Jan, will you come over at once. A story conference."

"I'll be right there," I said.

In fact, I did not see much of Louis over the next weeks. Although the studio was bullish about *Boomerang!*, which promised to be a winner (as indeed it was), the script conferences on *Spoonhandle* had run into difficulties. Louis and Darryl Zanuck did not see eye to eye over the development of the story. Both were strong personalities; terse memos passed to and fro, and Dick Murphy, caught in the crossfire, was involved in repeated rewrites.

In the meantime, having seen and learned as much as I could at Fox Hills, I hired a large Chevrolet and decided to cast my net wider, with visits to Walt Disney, in the San Fernando Valley, and to RKO and Technicolor.

Perhaps the one thing that had most fired my imagination about Hollywood was the showing in our local cinema in St. Andrews while I was still at school of Clemence Dane's *Bill of Divorcement*. It was Katharine Hepburn's first picture, and calf love or not, I could at least take credit in recognizing an entirely exceptional actress. I was determined to meet her now that I was actually there, and I discovered that she was starring in a musical epic, *Song of Love*, at Metro-Goldwyn-Mayer.

They had built the largest camera ramp in Hollywood history for the picture, rising from floor level to roof across the two largest sound stages at the studio. Invoking my fellowship and Rank connections, I obtained an introduction to Howard Strickling, head of publicity for the studio and right-hand man of Louis B. Mayer. He obligingly agreed to my request to inspect this technical miracle.

Ars Gratia Artis

"If only they came back as fast as they go out. The whole place empty in two minutes! Maybe we ought to eat on the set and shoot in the commissary." So commented Clarence Brown, producer and director of *Song of Love*. He looks ruefully at the disappearing extras.

All morning they have submitted to the commands of the loudspeaker, clapped their white-gloved hands, thrown posies of flowers, sat through the music as if entranced, and applauded with superhuman gusto.

"Bravo, bravo!" shouted the rotund little fellow with the mutton-chop whiskers standing next to me. "Bravo!" he shouted as if his very existence depended upon it—and indeed it does. They are paid fourteen bucks a day, I am told. Fourteen bucks for the dowager with the tiara, for that distinguished-looking general with the medals across his breast and the red braid down his trousers, fourteen bucks for a cardinal with a red hat.

"How much do you pay in England?" asks the prop in the red and black lumber jacket on my other side. I say that it is a pound a day at home—four dollars.

If you look closely, the fourteen-dollar magnificence ends at a predetermined level, generally near the bottom of the trousers. The camera cannot see their feet, least of all through the side of an opera box. Even Miss Hepburn, up there on the stage in a black dress, wears brown moccasins.

High above the roof of Stage Five, where they are shooting, stands a neon-lit lion and beneath it the words *Ars Gratia Artis*. It feels a little strange to be an Englishman in the lion's den and to be watching an actress for whom those words are not simply a trademark. She sits up there at the piano looking frail and old, and is playing in Dresden before the king and queen. (She explains afterward that they have drawn together the skin of her hands and face with rubber cement, and she wears a white wig.)

When she is not playing her part, her restless energy bursts through the artifice of the makeup man. There is a swing of the skirts that is Broadway and Ethel Merman.

"Yeah, yeah, yeah," she jerks at Clarence Brown. "And then do I cross in front of the camera? Yeah, I see. Don't you want a big glorious head? What, no big glorious head!" She breaks off. "Somebody give me a Lucky Strike." She cannot light it herself because of the elaborate makeup on her hands. Now *she* is telling Clarence Brown, "Oughtn't there to have been a light on my chin? There ought to have been a light." Who's directing the picture anyway, Hepburn or Brown? They laugh; he understands her very well.

Now, long dress or not, she has swung on to the camera boom and is chaffing the assistant. "These quiet men—I bet he's a real devil at home." She rocks with laughter.

It is time to rehearse, and the stage is cleared. The piano is out of position. Wait for a prop? Not she. The slim, black figure jumps up and pushes the Bechstein halfway across the stage.

"We oughta strike!" grumbles the hefty at my shoulder. Hepburn, a little breathless, gathers herself up and smiles.

There is a "burp, burp" from a loudspeaker and then the liquid notes of Schumann. She begins to play. The music comes from the speaker, but her hands finger the keyboard in exact time. "I didn't even know what an octave was when I began the picture," she says later on, but she had practiced for months.

She gets up, curtsies toward the royal box, and begins to speak. The shot is finished, and she has no more lines, but Clarence Brown has not said "cut." She grimaces, makes a graceful movement of interrogation with her hands.

It was when those extras had gone, in a flurry of bare shoulders, satin, lace, and gilt uniforms, that I saw the real actress. The great soundstage, with the huge ramp descending from the topmost gallery to the platform, is empty now except for a group gathered around the piano and microphone. The arc lights throw a hard, white light into the empty boxes through the criss-crossed scaffolding. She is a lonely figure by the piano—a great lady, I feel.

She is to step forward toward the royal box, say a few halting words, and sit down at the piano. I see now that she is taut.

"Will you *please* keep quiet behind there. I may be very old now, but I still hear very well." She smiles and we laugh. She advances, presses her hands together and begins, "Your majesties, ladies and gentlemen, it is so long now . . . I, I . . . so good . . ." At first I think the tears are artificial, but they are not. Her voice takes on the quavering quality of an old woman's.

"May I do it again, Clarence?" and Clarence Brown moves over, pats her on the back, and gives a word or two of advice.

Before she begins again, she appeals to the crew to keep absolutely still. "It's so difficult to do," she says. All is quiet now.

"Camera," shouts Brown.

Then with a gesture of the hands, she says, "I'm sorry, you'll have to come out of there," and the unit manager and head cameraman are bundled from the vantage point where they had caught her eye.

She says her lines perfectly; her bosom swells, she clenches her hands; her words would wring tears from a rock. "It's all right, is it?" and with a generosity that includes the whole crew in her achievement, "I knew we had it."

And there I lose her. She comes down afterward, and I watch her out of the tail of my eye, as my friend in the lumber jacket asks me about British film production. I speak to her briefly, but already the miles of sea to England are opening before me. The tall, black figure recedes, the questions I am too shy to ask will go unanswered, and I am left with a sense of personal loss.

I duly submitted this piece to Howard Strickling, who withheld permission to publish it. He said that the sketch of Katharine Hepburn was not sufficiently glamorous—and perhaps felt that I should have confined myself to the camera ramp. It was later printed in England under the title of "Don't, Mr. Editor," and Miss Hepburn wrote me to say that she liked it. Through no fault of hers or her performance, *Song of Love* was not the best of her films, *Time* commenting ironically, "This is how Brahms and the Schumanns might very possibly have acted if they had realized that later on they would break into movies."

Years later, my wife and I wrote a book called *The Great British Breakfast* and, hearing that she approved of British breakfasts, I sent her a copy through my agents. Most people, and especially stars, absorb books without a thank you, but Katharine Haughton Hepburn wrote to us, "What fun the book. And how nice of you to think of me. Thank you and your wife very much."

By this time I was settling into a pleasant life in Beverly Hills. Apart from an unheard-of snow shower in late January, the sun shone every day—smog was not the problem that it is now—and the girls walked about the streets in bikinis. Since the small Beverly House hotel had no restaurant, I used to breakfast al fresco at a nearby café, Parker's Grill and Griddle, at a table flanked by orange trees in tubs and off glasses of fresh Californian orange juice. It was owned by the Marx brothers, and from time to time Groucho, minus his painted black moustache, showed up to check on the takings.

Beverly Hills was, in fact, very much a village community, though if of an evening, so as to get a little exercise, I walked down Rodeo Drive, with its swank houses and well-watered lawns so reminiscent of Raymond Chandler (I actually heard the shots the night that Bugsy Siegel was murdered), I was inevitably picked up by a police car and driven to my destination, the Beverly Hills Hotel. Using one's legs was an English habit the Los Angeles cops could never understand.

In a bookshop in Beverly Hills, of all places, I even found a first edition of Joseph Conrad's *Nostromo* for a few dollars and began scripting it to occupy my spare time, but my undemanding routine was now abruptly interrupted.

I was sitting at my typewriter one afternoon in the Beverly House hotel when Louis, unannounced and in a high state of excitement, irrupted into the room with half a dozen of his aides. The little hotel can never have seen such turmoil. It transpired that he had walked out of 20th Century–Fox and come hot-foot from the studio to my hotel on its doorstep to make long-distance calls to his agent, his attorney, and other associates in New York.

The discussions on *Spoonhandle* had taken a dramatic turn for the worse. The book revolved around two brothers from a small town on the coast of New England, one of whom wished to continue the traditional business of fishing and the other to develop the place as a dormitory for well-heeled New Yorkers. Darryl Zanuck tossed in the suggestion that the parts of the brothers be combined. Louis countered this with a long and thoughtfully argued memo, pointing out that the whole raison d'être for the story would be lost if there was no conflict between the brothers. To this, Zanuck had tersely replied, "How would it be if Hamlet were brothers?"

It was at this point that Louis resigned.

Whatever the rights and wrongs of this argument, Zanuck was one of the most impressive of all Hollywood producers. Like other omnipotent studio bosses of the time, I have heard him described on television as a "monster." This is grotesque. Authoritarian he certainly was, and he ruled his producers with a rod of iron. A small man and physically unimpressive, he fostered this impression by striding purposefully about the studio in breeches and riding boots. He is perhaps best known for grooming a succession of decorative blondes, from Alice Faye and Betty Grable to Marilyn Monroe, for the glossy 20th Century–Fox musicals. However, he first came to the top at Warner Brothers, which of all the Hollywood studios specialized in making factual biographies, such as *Pasteur* and *Zola*, and raw crime pictures like *I Am a Fugitive from a Chain Gang*, depicting the more down-to-earth aspects of American life.

It was 20th Century–Fox under Zanuck and Skouras that was bold enough to take on *The March of Time*, so it was hardly coincidental that he backed Louis de Rochemont's experiments in semidocumentary and the shooting of entertainment pictures on location, long before this became general practice. Unlike many of the front-office moguls, he was also a thoroughly practical filmmaker and a brilliant editor—many an ailing Fox picture was saved by Zanuck's intervention in the cutting room.

The row over *Spoonhandle*, though a clean break at the time, did not end his relations with Louis. Much later, after Zanuck had left Hollywood to make *The Longest Day*, about the D-day landings, Louis phoned me requesting my urgent presence in Paris—more, I suspect, to bring him supplies of Harrod's smoked salmon and Antiquary whiskey than for any help I could give him on his current film. There, at a restaurant near the Pont Royale Hotel, we came on Darryl Zanuck, who had recently split from the singer Juliette Greco, solitary and *triste* at a table by himself, and we joined him for a most amicable meal.

When the dust over *Spoonhandle* had subsided a bit, Louis managed to extricate himself from his Fox contract, but only on condition that he make no feature picture for any other company for an agreed period. His thoughts now turned to a project that he had been nursing for some time, a series of geographical pictures, and his one thought was to shake the dust of Hollywood off his feet.

Naturally, I was affected by the general debacle; my Fox expense allowance was abruptly terminated, and as an immediate economy I handed back the Chevrolet. In spite of his own troubles, Louis, in his big-hearted way, did not forget my own predicament. As it happened, Pictorial Research, Inc., was about to begin a film for the Insurance Company of North America, shooting sequences coast to coast with the idea of interesting prospective employees in the excitements of the life of an insurance salesman.

The crew consisted of a young documentary director and former child star, Phil de Lacey, and myself, and it reminded me very much of my days with the Strand Film Company in Cornwall. We duly set out in the de Rochemonts' large Chrysler station wagon, with a large pottery kiln for Ginnie occupying the rear, taking turns at driving and going by way of the Mojave Desert, Phoenix, El Paso, the Panhandle of Texas, Dallas, St. Louis, down the Pennsylvania Turnpike to Philadelphia, the headquarters of the corporation, and on to New York. When we made a stopover for filming we would draw on the local newsreel outfit for a cameraman and equipment.

The first port of call was a golf course in Santa Monica, where the local insurance rep was supposed to disport himself, and where to my surprise I found that the pro was one of the Aytons whose brother Laurie had coached me in St. Andrews. Our most memorable sequence was shot in a snowbound St. Louis. For most of the four-thousand-mile journey we lodged at wayside motels, but here we spent a week at the palatial Sports Club and filmed on a snow-covered waste outside the city, as one of the men from the St. Louis office of the insurance company pretended to assess its suitability as an airfield.

It was a memorable journey—almost cut short when speeding down the empty main street of Tucson I was pulled up by a motorcycle cop, who asked where I thought was going. I innocently said New York, and but for some fast talk by Phil would have landed up not there but in the local jail.

CHAPTER FOUR

125th Street

We arrived in New York in early March; it was wet and windy, and in my straitened circumstances I managed to find a small room in International House, a hostel on 125th Street run by Columbia University for graduate students from overseas. It was a far cry from the heady existence in Hollywood; Louis was depressed and not very well and had as yet not been able to get his other schemes under way, so I occupied myself as best I could with my typewriter.

James Thurber once remarked that literature is born of a modicum of thought and a lot of looking out of the window, and I spent more time looking out over the grey Hudson River than in writing. Across on the Jersey bank there was first the Palisade Amusement Park, then the big neon sign over the Ford wharf, and farthest downstream the Spry sign. It was this, with its changing message "Spry for Baking," "Spry for Frying," and finally just "Spry," that engaged me hypnotically when I was stuck for an idea.

Deciding to start at the top, I set to work on a piece destined for *The New Yorker*. It was inspired by visits to Café Society downtown with Hugh Lester, the publicity man, during my palmier days on *Boomerang!*; Sally Rand, the bubble dancer, was then performing there. When I finished it, I felt that the argot was not all that it should be and took it to

Alistair Cooke, who always had time for younger Commonwealth Fund Fellows like myself. Entering into the spirit of the story, he sat down with me at a table by the Rockefeller Center skating rink and blue-penciled the dialogue.

The Man Who Ate Pretzels

Minelli's Café is in the fifties west of Broadway. It is a quiet little place used mainly by show people. You go down two wooden steps into a long passage of a room with the bar along one side and a dozen or two tables beyond, each with its red and white check cloth. Joe Minelli, a fat good-humored man, his thinning hair plastered greasily over the back of his head, sits at the cash register, just next to the bar and opposite the juke box. Occasionally he'll get up and by some sleight of hand release from the box a torrent of nickels, half of which he pockets, feeding back the other half into the machine, so that it lights up and the colored bubbles chase round its bulbous front while the voice of Perry Como rolls around the room.

I am sitting at the bar one evening reading *Variety*, when in comes a character who takes the stool next to mine. It seems he's well known in the joint, because Sam, the barman, mixes him a Scotch and soda and hauls out a bowl of pretzels from under the counter.

"Hiya," says Sam, who's a friendly guy, "What's new?"

But the stranger just nods and doesn't answer. I don't say anything, because I am just in from Atlantic City, and I want to get up to date. "Nudity Return Noted in N.Y. Cafes," I read on the front page of *Variety*. Makes sense, I figure, if it saves four-hundred dollars per costume and the flesh displays lure the out-of-town trade into the cafés.

I don't drink fast, because I turn the pages and read about the plight of the "Wheel 'Em-Deak 'Em Boys" in Las Vegas. Seems there's less walk-around money from Hollywood; the blue jays are laying nuts for the winter. Too bad, I think: with the boys from the studios quitting blackjack and craps, that Mike Goetz who just opened a night spot in the desert is gonna lose an awful wad of cabbage.

I finish my glass of rye and I notice the stranger is drinking Scotch like it's piped and eats pretzels like a lizard snapping flies. When he goes to the men's room, I say to Sam: "For cryin' out loud! Who is this pretzel-eating character?"

"He comes in every night," Sam says. "Used to eat here too, then he stops sudden and only eats pretzels."

The guy turns to me when he comes back and as soon as he opens his trap I know he's a limey. "May I look at your paper?" he says. He's a tall mournful-looking guy, and I see for the first time that he wears a tuxedo under his coat.

"Sure," I says. "Go right ahead."

He reads for a few minutes while I order me another rye, then he points to the paper and says in an English voice that sounds like he has a hot potato in his mouth, "That's how I lost my job." And he looks at me and takes a grab at the pretzels.

"How come?" I ask, and he points to the spread about the return of nudity to the New York cafés.

I read it again, but I don't see any names I ain't familiar with. "What they call you?" I ask.

"Cyril Beaumont," he says.

"There's no Cyril Beaumont here."

"Well, it's like this," he answers. "Mayor LaGuardia put burlesque out of business, but the article says that the café proprietors reckon the police have cooled off since then. They were optimists, because our show was raided last week."

"Where d'you work?"

"At Billy Cantor's," he says.

Then I remember that the day I leave for Atlantic City, Billy Cantor calls me at the agency looking for talent. It seems the cops have nixed the strip act at his Rio Tinto Club. "They sit there all night," he tells me, "expending the public funds on liquor. They sit at the ringside. Slipped Walter"—he's the headwaiter at Billy's joint—"a ten-dollar bill. They lamp the show all night, dinner *and* supper. They sit there until Judy sees those boys are inarrested and natchally she favors them. I don't say she's unfair to the other customers; she shows them all she can, but those boys she's shows plenty. And when Cyril does his act, they step in. And that," says Billy, "is how the cops in this town spend the taxpayers' dough."

Now Billy's a good boy and I don't like to see a good boy go wrong, so I peddle him what I got and it costs him plenty. I like to help a guy, but you gotta live. But to come back to this mournful pretzel-eating British character, I still don't get it. He don't look like he's ever seen a strip. Why in heck would a juvenile in burlesque go around wearing a tuxedo?

"See here," I says, and I'm really interested, "I don't get it. Better take another and give us the story."

"Well," says the British character, taking a handful of pretzels, "It's like this. After I left Oxford, I joined the Cudworth Repertory Company and when the call came I went to the West End. I preferred playing in Shakespeare."

I began to see a light. "You weren't in that limey outfit off Broadway that just folded?"

He nods gloomily and Joe breaks in. "We know that Shakespeare's strictly class—but what's it to do with pretzels or strippers?"

"Hold it, boy," I says. "Give him time, he's getting there. The same all round, Sam."

"No," says Joe, "this round's on the house. Make it a double for our English friend, Sam, and get him some more pretzels." Then Joe goes over to the Wurlitzer, and the nickels rattle out like it's a piggy bank. Joe starts it again, and we all look at the Englishman.

"To come straight to the point," he says, "I was stranded in New York without a job. My funds were running low and I was sitting one evening at a table in the Rio Tinto. I'd put on the dinner jacket because I thought, well, if we're going to perish, let's perish gloriously. I thought I'd have to pawn it next day. Now I figured I had just enough for six Scotch and sodas, but I'd forgotten the cover charge, so when the waiter came with the bill I hadn't enough to pay. He fetched the proprietor, but instead of getting angry, Mr. Cantor looked me up and down and said: 'I've a proposition to make.'"

"Trust Billy," I says.

"He looked at me," the pretzel-monger continues, "and said, 'That's a nice number you're wearing.' 'Like to buy it?' I asked, 'You can have it cheap.' 'No,' said Mr. Cantor, 'but maybe I can use you in my show? Ever acted?' I told him how I was fixed and he said: 'You're signed right now. Ten bucks a night.' 'Ten dollars?' I said, 'but what on earth do I do?' 'Just sit here and watch the show,' Mr. Cantor said, 'until I give you your cue.'"

"Give him another drink," I whisper to Sam, but Sam is so interested he doesn't hear me. "Ten bucks a night," he says, "for sitting in a tuxedo and watching a striptease. Boy, why am I slinging drinks?"

"Well, after all," I says, "it ain't just our English friend. There's the tuxedo too."

"Say, fella," says Sam, "like to sell the tuxedo?"

"Delighted," says the Englishman, "but I think it's only fair to tell you how it ended."

"Sure," I says, "Go right ahead."

"I thought the show was very daring. First there was a beauty chorus, and they weren't overdressed. Then the lights were dimmed, and Judy came on wearing a loose muslin dress and did some classical dances—but that didn't last long."

"Trust Billy," I says. "Go ahead."

"Yes," says the Englishman, "the dress seemed suddenly to disappear, and then she was wearing very little at all, except that she had some large green balloons which she kept floating in front of her."

"Yeah, go on," says Joe, pushing over the pretzels.

"Well, I thought that was enough for anybody, but not for Mr. Cantor. I suddenly felt his hand on my shoulder. 'Take your cigarette,' he said, 'and burst them balloons.'"

"Well, *that's* a gimmick," I says. "That's really for the book. I guess the ten bucks bailed you out?"

"Yes, they threw me out each night, but it was worth it. You can buy a lot for ten dollars," and he looks past Sam at the bottles.

"But the pretzels?" says Joe.

"Oh, that's obvious. When the show closed, I had to choose between eating and Scotch. Well, pretzels are all you get free in New York, so I eat pretzels."

My plight was not, of course, quite as bad as my hero's, and International House was, in fact, a most fascinating place, a melting pot of cultures from the seven quarters of the globe. It overlooks the Hudson on Riverside Drive and 125th Street on the fringes of Harlem. The famous Cotton Club, venue of Duke Ellington, Cab Calloway, and "Bojangles" Robinson had closed a few years before, and when we wanted to hear jazz we fared downtown to Greenwich Village, but the district was still lively, not the least of its attractions being the numerous Chinese restaurants, where one ate well and, as importantly, cheaply.

One found one's own level among the hundreds of graduate students who had come to study science, sociology, economics, American history—or drama . . .

Natalia

Of course everybody at the hostel knows Natalia, at least by sight and repute: Natalia of the prune-dark eyes and torrential Spanish, Natalia who stands out from the ruck like a mountain peak from the level of a plain.

In an amateur way I had even investigated the subject of Natalia. I would observe her come down to breakfast in a gauzy spring frock; by lunchtime she might be wearing a pink wool dress; for dinner, a black evening gown, a white wrap and the sheerest of nylon stockings; and later, for supper, a green dress with embroidered flowers. Someone told me that she came from Venezuela and was the daughter of a powerful politico. I didn't doubt it; so superb a creature could spring from a setting no less romantic. You may judge that even by this early date I was far from being untouched by Natalia, because I had gone so far as to compose the opening lines of a poem in her honor. Nothing less than poetry can really describe her.

Well, I was sitting between Natalia and a tiresome woman with frizzled hair who kept drooling on about *Monsieur Verdoux*, the new Chaplin film. "I never liked Charlie Chaplin or Maurice Chevalier," she was saying, as if Chaplin and Chevalier were brothers in arms, "I never did, not even in my school days." I thought what a long, long time ago that must have been.

However, just to annoy Natalia, who cannot bear being left out, I pretended to be deeply interested. She turned to me and at once, with the most palpable flattery, caught me hook, line, and sinker. In two minutes I was following her to the coffee bar as securely in tow as if I had been chained to her, and as I asked for one black coffee and one with cream and sugar, I heard myself issuing an invitation to the Chaplin film in question. Ten minutes later I was pacing the lobby in a freshly pressed suit and wondering what new dress I might expect her in. I give these details just to illustrate the surprising reactions that Natalia evokes. As the young man with whom she "goes" remarked one breakfast time when the sun got in our eyes, "What between Natalia and the sun."

I think she must like English people, because she is going to the Royal Academy of Dramatic Art in London this fall, and perhaps she found in my Anglo-Saxon reticence a foil to her own excitability. At any rate, we walked in the dark past Grant's Tomb down to the Fifth Avenue bus, and neither of us felt the least incongruity. As the bus lumbers downtown, I should explain that Natalia is more than a student of the theater; she is the self-constituted savior of the Venezuelan stage. She plans to restore to their rightful places the Knight of the Sorrowful Countenance, the poetry of Lorca, the drama of Calderón de la Barca; but more than this, she will bring to the Spanish theater, if she had to write them herself, epics of the present day, real, throbbing, stark.

It surprised me that she talked to me once she found that I had been working as assistant to a Hollywood producer. "Holleewood!" she exclaimed with a scornful toss of her head. "You pretend to despise eet, and you seem so fascinated with eet." (I can only attempt to indicate Natalia's entirely individualistic English.) "Don't worry, it's where you'll end up too, Natalia," I said. "Now that Carmen Miranda has left 20th Century–Fox, they could do with you." "Carmen Miranda!" she exploded, half-angry, half-laughing. I guess it was that chance remark that drew us together; anyway, I liked her for her passionate convictions, for charging windmills so heroically and laughing at herself afterward.

We got off the bus at 53rd Street and walked toward the Broadway Theater, Natalia stopping for a moment to look into the brightly lit Museum of Modern Art, as if to demonstrate her solidarity with such a high-minded venture, if only by this little gesture. As we walked along, we swapped yarns about London and Caracas, and she spoke about England with a kind of wistfulness and respect. I wondered how she visualized it and hoped she would reach London in the spring and not, I hoped, in the drizzle of a wet November. Thinking of the polite astonishment with which the English would most likely receive her, I decided that I had better give her my telephone number in case she grew dispirited. At any rate, by the time I put down my money at the box office, we had agreed that both London and Caracas were much better soil for the artist than dollar-ridden New York.

She really seemed as much interested in the newsreel of Henry Wallace as in Charlie Chaplin, and lest you should think that Natalia walks with her head in the clouds, I may add that she once wrote articles for a socialist newspaper. After the show she told me so herself over a highball in the Trianon Room. She looked at me very solemnly, her round face framed by her black, glossy hair. "You think," she said, "that I am not serious minded. In Caracas it is different. There, I think in Spanish and write in Spanish. English is still a foreign language to me, and I cannot say what I want."

I saw Natalia, or tried to see her, in my mind's eye, spreading the inflammatory doctrines around the sun-baked streets and plaza of Caracas, high on its hilltop.

"You wouldn't like to dance, would you?" I asked.

"Of course, if you want to," she said with a trace of surprise in her voice, as if it astonished her that an Englishman should suggest anything so abandoned.

"And what," I said, taking hold of her possessively, for Natalia is very nice to dance with, "does your family think about socialism?"

"Oh, *they,* they do not like it. They belong to the opposite party. They did not want me to become an actress, but when my party came into power I was given a scholarship to come to New York."

"Then you're sitting pretty. When your party's in power, *they* look after you, and when they're out, your parents do." Natalia laughed and I went on. "I didn't know there *were* any socialists in South America. I thought it was just a struggle between different landowners."

"Perhaps in other countries," she said, "not in mine."

We sat down and had another drink, and later Natalia returned to the subject. "I was never an extreme socialist," she said dreamily and looked around the luxurious restaurant. "I like to be a socialist and keep my maids to press my dresses and lay them out." She looked at me thoughtfully and laughed. "Can I be a socialist and want that? It is very difficult here in New York without a maid. I live a, what do you call it, the Spartan life."

At that I could easily have embraced Natalia, because I so entirely saw her point—I had spent so much time just wondering what her room must be like after the white dress had given place to the pink one, the pink to the red, the red to the black, the black to the green one with the Indian embroidery, and the green embroidered one to the brown evening gown—and that's leaving out lots of others and all her sweaters and Scots tartans.

"I may not be a very good socialist," she said with a flashing smile, "but I have a big heart!"

I cannot remember which dress she was wearing when I next saw her at the hostel; all I do recall is that she was bare-legged and had on a pair of old but beautifully embroidered black slippers. She was full of *Weldschmerz* and in a submissive mood—for Natalia. I think she was cast down over her progress in the English language and more particularly over *Idiot's Delight,* which is to be her test piece for an audition in England. She confessed to me that the world was in a very sorry state and that there was nothing much that she or I could do about it—except go and live in the country and look at things that grow under the sky. I guess we are both painters at heart, and while I saw Ludlow and the castle framed by dark-green horse chestnuts, she was in the emptiness of the savannas.

"I'm part Indian," she said, as if to complete my thought.

"And what else are you?"

"Spanish mostly, part Irish, part French."

"That explains everything," I laughed, and Natalia took her serviette and carefully dabbed her lips so that the lipstick left two heart-shaped marks on the crinkly paper.

"I suppose that's how you mark your victims," said I.

Her face, I could see now, was more than a little Indian, the chin especially—but then again, I once knew an Irish girl with that squarish sort of face—and into her eyes there climbed the faintest trace of suspicion and doubt.

"No," she said soberly, "I'm not that sort of woman. I don't need kiss-proof lipstick."

So we just talked for a time until she got up, and in a manner born of perfect breeding—alas, too seldom found in the hostel—she said, "Thank you for your company."

A week or two later, I returned to Hollywood, and I do not know whether Natalia has really gone to England. Perhaps I shall pick up the phone some day in London and out of it will shower Natalia's English; or perhaps, years ahead, I shall be sitting on one side of a desk in a movie company's office and in will stalk Natalia, ten times more glamorous and half as lovely, sporting that weakness of hers for a new dress and coming to ask for the Carmen Miranda part in our latest super-colossal Latin American musical. I hope not. I'd much rather read about her as the rising star of the reborn Venezuelan theater.

In fact, I was to see a lot more of Natalia Silva Bermúdez, to give her her full name. We soon discovered a mutual interest in jazz and began going together to the Village Vanguard or Eddie Condon's to listen to the likes of Lee Wiley, Peewee Russell, or Bud Freeman; she even, in the face of stiff competition, decided that I should escort her to the International House ball.

She *did* go to the Royal Academy of Dramatic Art, and the next time I heard from her was when the telephone rang in London and an excited Natalia asked if I and my cousin would be the witnesses at the Kensington Registry Office when she married a journalist from *Realités*, a handsome ex-pilot from the Free French Air Force. I would visit them at their apartment near the Bois de Boulogne in Paris, then lost touch for some years, only to rediscover her remarried and producing Lope de Vega in Madrid, of which more later.

I took time off from Natalia and the typewriter to look up some of the small band of documentary filmmakers in New York—among others Irving Jacoby, Henwar Rodakiewicz, and Willard Van Dyke—to whom Paul Rotha had given me letters of introduction. The charming and troubled Iris Barry, an English expatriate, gave me the run of the film library at the Museum of Modern Art, and John Grierson, who was by now head of the film division of UNESCO, suggested that if I had time on my hands I might care to work on a documentary he was producing in Canada. I was more interested, on meeting Helen van Dongen, cutter for the legendary Robert Flaherty (maker of *Nanook of the North* and *Elephant Boy*), to hear that he was beginning a new picture in the swamps of Louisiana. She thought he might like to have me on the unit, and I wrote off at once, only to receive a charming reply saying that that he would have been delighted but that the small boat on which they were living was already bursting at the seams.

Always at the back of my mind was the thought that my first loyalty lay with Louis de Rochemont, but there were no signs of his protracted negotiations with United World Pictures over the geographical series being brought to a conclusion. He kept silence for weeks at a time in his lair at the Waldorf. Meanwhile the cherry trees broke into blossom along Riverside Drive, and the sands of my fellowship were running out.

I still had one ace to play, a letter from J. Arthur Rank to Nate Blumberg, the president of Universal Pictures, and I turned again to the energetic Colonel Lawrence. Jock counseled me to return to Hollywood and use the letter—as it happened, he was about to leave for the coast himself.

First and most difficult was to break the news to Louis. Attached to him as I was and deeply indebted for all that he had done, I knew all too well that he was possessive to a degree and that the idea of my returning to Hollywood would result in an instant explosion. In the event I decided it best to write him the nicest possible letter, which I delivered by hand at the Waldorf.

The result, of course, was an immediate telephone call.

"Jan," began the deep voice vibrating with rage, "I think that was a stinking letter you wrote me . . ."

When I had taken the punishment I looked around the room, limp and played out. The books were in their accustomed places, the towels across the radiator, there was even a copy of that letter lying on the table. I went to the window and looked across the river. "Spry for Baking," "Spry for Frying," "Spry," the sign spelled out. They had even replaced the missing B of "Baking." I suppose, I thought vaguely, they have a stock of the things and a breakdown gang. How easy for them to make repairs!

Fortunately, this was far from being the end of the story. I worked on scripts for Louis as long as he made films, writing additional dialogue for the last feature picture that he and Vivien Leigh were to make together, *The Roman Spring of Mrs. Stone*. Over the years, one never knew when Louis de Rochemont's commanding voice would break from the phone, whether from across the Atlantic or from the Carlton Tower hotel next door to us in London.

He was a big man in every sense, an innovator who stood up for what he believed in, was devoted to his family and New England, and was generous and very human too. I can still see his large figure hand in hand with our infant son, leading the way into the Rib Room at the Carlton Tower. There were raised eyebrows when the tot asked for fish and chips with *gravy*. Louis summoned the headwaiter and said in a voice that brooked no refusal: "Captain, pour him some gravy from the end of the roast."

CHAPTER FIVE

∼

Hollywood, Reel 2

Just as with the airlines today, there was fierce competition between the different railroads with services from the East to Los Angeles. The Northern Pacific played up the scenic attractions of its route, with the bonus of a run along the Pacific from Seattle; as a compensation for changing at St. Louis, the Rock Island Railroad offered double-decker observation coaches. The Southern Pacific, which took four days for the journey, held out a stopover in New Orleans with time to explore the old French Quarter—on my return journey I took advantage of this to visit the jazz joints and sample the oysters with the famous green sauce at Antoine's. Right now, as I was impatient to get back and had already ridden the Santa Fe, I plumped for the direct route of the Union Pacific via Salt Lake City.

Without my Fox expense allowance, I looked for inexpensive accommodation once I arrived. Another Commonwealth Fund Fellow, Ian Watt (subsequently the illustrious professor of humanities at Stanford University), suggested that I move into a basement garage that he was sharing with a couple of graduates of the Department of Theater Arts at UCLA.

It was in Laurel Canyon just down from the house of Henry Miller, author of *Air-Conditioned Nightmare*. The precipitous canyon was then, as now, a community of its own, with a single general store in the middle, where we bought carboys of Californian wine and all our other provisions. Every morning, while we were still asleep, a uniformed delivery man would walk in with blocks of ice to replenish the antique ice chest. The company was stimulating, but after a week of sleeping on an old davenport I decided that I must settle somewhere more accessible to launch my new attack on the studios and moved back into my old quarters in the Beverly House Hotel.

My first port of call was to Universal to enlist the help of Colonel Lawrence, whom I found in his office, shirt-sleeved as usual with the scarlet braces, in the thick of making arrangements for a more important visitor—no less than J. Arthur Rank in person. Apart from Nate Blumberg, the studio bosses at the time were Leo Spitz, Ben Goetz, and Bill Dozier. Surprisingly, Jock was himself typing laboriously; he looked up to quip, "In this studio they wear out all the Zs on the typewriters."

We discussed my own small affairs, and he promised, once Mr. Rank was on his way, to ring me at the hotel. I had almost given up hope of hearing from him and was taking up the script of *Nostromo,* which I had started months before in the same room, when the telephone rang, and he asked me to go over at once to Universal. This time he had with him a tall man with greying hair, erect and soldierly, and wearing a monocle. Jock introduced us. "I'd like you to meet Fritz Lang."

I, of course, was only too well aware of the achievements of the great director, beginning with his classic German films—the *Siegfried* cycle, *Metropolis,* M, and the others. At a very early age I remember seeing *Metropolis* in the Old Cinema House in St. Andrews with a couple of school friends and, when their mother decided that it was unsuitable for young children, refusing to leave the cinema with them.

As the Nazis extended their stranglehold to the German cinema, Lang, together with other expatriates, such as Marlene Dietrich and Otto Preminger, had departed for Hollywood. He told me later that Hitler had in fact suggested that he become *Führer* of the German film industry, but he was in no doubts about his decision to leave. After making fine pictures at M-G-M like *Fury,* with Spencer Tracy, and *You Only Live Once,* with Henry Fonda, Lang had migrated to Universal, setting up his own production company, Diana Film Productions, with Walter Wanger and his wife, Joan Bennett (the company was, in fact, named after Joan's daughter).

Diana had made the intriguing and very successful *Woman in the Window,* starring Joan Bennett and Edward G. Robinson, and Lang was now completing another picture, *The Secret beyond the Door.* It again starred

Joan Bennett, and, by arrangement with Rank, Michael Redgrave had been brought from England to play opposite her. The shrewd Colonel Lawrence sensed that Lang and Wanger might like to strengthen their ties with the J. Arthur Rank Organisation by taking me on.

The introductions over, Fritz walked me down to the bungalow at the far end of the lot occupied by Diana and interrogated me in more detail. He was somewhat formidable on first acquaintance; I remember the diplomatic Walter Wanger did his best to put me at my ease and that Diana's third director, the darkly beautiful Joan Bennett, looked in briefly to cast her eye over me. In the upshot, Fritz said that I was welcome to learn what I could on the stages, in the cutting room, and at script conferences, and hearing that I was an aspiring writer, asked if I could help him with the scores of articles for which he received incessant requests from magazines and newspapers.

Universal, situated near Walt Disney's in the San Fernando Valley across a pass in the Hollywood Hills, was a sprawling assemblage of offices and soundstages, many of them dating from the time they were first built to make silent films. The low front office was still surmounted by a pole, on which in the days of the studio's founder, Carl Laemle, a flag had been run up when the sun was bright enough for shooting on the open-air sets. The back lot was one of the largest in Hollywood, its main feature being the extended standing set of the main street in a western township, complete with the fronts of houses, hotels, banks, hitching posts, and saloons with swinging bat-wing doors. Since the silent era this had regularly been revamped (as it still is) for making westerns, not only by Universal but also by other studios.

The independent producers working under Universal's umbrella occupied air-conditioned bungalows farther back. Ours stood next to one with the shingle "S. P. Eagle"—this was before the redoubtable Sam reverted to his native name of Spiegel. It was like stepping into a furnace to leave our cool office and walk the quarter of a mile to the commissary during the Californian summer.

Diana Productions was a tight ship. Fritz Lang occupied a roomy suite furnished with large, black leather settees, green-shuttered against the fierce sun and usually in a state of subaqueous half-light. Silvia Richards, who had written the script of *Secret beyond the Door* and was now at work on the next production, *Winchester 73* (which for reasons I do not know was produced and directed not by Fritz Lang but by Anthony Mann), produced her daily quota of pages in a tiny cubbyhole, while I was assigned a desk and typewriter in the general office, which housed Fritz's executive assistant, Min Selvin, and his secretary, Hilda Rolfe, a willowy and gentle girl with a Madonna-like face and long black hair. As was the custom, the other "indies"—cutters, cameramen, assistant directors, and all the rest of the numerous crew—were hired from Universal when a film was actually on the floor.

To begin with, I spent as much time as possible on the set, in the cutting room, and watching the previous day's rushes in a projection theater.

Drinking Straws

I never order a soda these days without thinking of them. The scene: a café in Mexico, stone flagged with iron tables, an old man in the background asleep over a newspaper, and the barman mixing drinks.

The girl, obviously a rich American, is carefully, or rather meticulously, dressed. There is not a crease on her gown, except for the creases that are intentional and look fresh from the iron. Her hair, divided evenly on either side of her shapely head, is jet black and glossy and sets off her dark, possessive eyes. She sits at the table taking a sip from the tall glass in front of her.

Then abruptly the man sits down beside her. He is in his shirtsleeves. His hair is brushed back from his forehead; he is altogether of most military appearance and wears glasses. He sits astride the chair and leans toward the girl, talking to her with great seriousness.

She smiles amusedly, then reaches for her glass to take a drink. He shakes his head and, glancing over his shoulder, calls the waiter. They sit in silence until the waiter puts down a glass on the table, a tall glass with two straws. He picks it up with great deliberation and drinks through the straws, then nods to her. She drinks, but he is uneasy and looks hurriedly around the café. The old gentleman still dozes behind his paper. The only noise is the tinkle of ice as the barman mixes drinks. A hard blue light falls across the empty tables.

He jumps up suddenly, as if he has made up his mind, and returns with a spool of Scotch tape. Then, taking the straws from her glass, he binds them securely together so that they no longer sprawl akimbo over the rim but stand straight with soldierly precision, with the same upright bearing as his own, now that he stands smiling and triumphant. "Shoot, my children, shoot!" Lang cries and watches as Joan Bennett drinks.

As shooting neared an end and Fritz was less preoccupied, I spent increasingly more time with him discussing the articles, for which, as he had said, he was inundated with requests, be it from the University of California's highbrow *Hollywood Quarterly* or *Theatre Arts,* the *Los Angeles Times,* or one of the Hollywood columnists.

The drill was for us to thrash out the content together; I would then sit down at the typewriter and produce a first draft, on which he would make detailed comments and suggestions in his firm, angular hand. The hour before lunch became sacrosanct. The pieces varied from the light and inconsequential, for Delight Evans or Virginia Wright, to the intellectual and academic, for *Hollywood Quarterly*. Each time we talked I learned something more about his attitude toward films, filmmaking, and drama—which he would illustrate by explaining why he had incorporated a sequence in M or *Metropolis* and how he had realized the effect he had been striving for.

He was, of course, a master of the macabre, and one of the first articles dealt with the psychology of the murderer. Others ranged from long pieces on censorship, on westerns and the real West, and, in lighter vein, on the pretensions of producers in *A Frog Defies Hollywood.*

To illustrate the points made in the articles—and because he evidently perceived my vivid interest—Fritz ran most of his old silent films for me at the studio, sitting with me and explaining how he had achieved the effects. For example, he described the days of shooting involved in Siegfried's battle with the dragon, large enough to accommodate a dozen men inside, who squeezed out a sticky fluid from large rubber bags as the hero pierced the monster with his lance.

As I grew to know him better, he often invited me to his house, perched on top of the Hollywood Hills with canyons falling away steeply on either side of a garden luxuriant with cactus and purple bougainvillea. With the monocle he sported on public occasions and his commanding manner, one might be excused for taking him for a Prussian military officer, but outward appearances belied a most complex personality embracing a passionate belief in democracy, a keen and subtle intellect, a flair for storytelling, an artist's eye for composition, and a feeling for the mystical and macabre. I think of him as a shy, and in many ways very lonely, man—he had separated from his wife when she became a Nazi.

In that garden, which seemed on top of the world, we had long discussions about painting, alchemy, Ibsen, Japanese miniatures, the foolishness of building houses on the sides of canyons, and above all on the art and craft of filmmaking. He was keen on wine and had a good cellar, both French and Californian, and we often tasted the wines side by side, agreeing that—the vineyards had not yet fully recovered from the effects of the Prohibition era—the Californian seemed somewhat "wooden" and uncomplex compared with the French. It was an unending dialogue, continued on occasion at the Brown Derby or Larue (then the most elegant restaurant on Sunset Strip). He was also an aficionado of the hot Mexican food and on visits to the Mexican village in downtown Los Angeles introduced me to tamales and enchiladas, and the correct way of drinking tequila, with a pinch of salt between thumb and forefinger.

I also became firm friends with Diana's resident scriptwriter, Silvia Richards, a courageous and outspoken girl with a mane of glorious red hair. She had been ditched abruptly by her husband—oddly enough, a producer at Louis de Rochemont's *March of Time*—with two small children on her hands. Without any experience she had thereupon carved out for herself a career as a successful scriptwriter. It often crossed my mind that there was a liaison between her and Fritz. I never knew for sure, but in many ways they seemed made for each other.

Min Selvin, the third member of the triumvirate at Diana, was an older woman, married to an official of one of the film unions, Norval Krutcher. She liked to describe herself and her husband as Hollywood radicals, and over king-sized prawn cocktails at the studio commissary she would enlighten me as to the feudal attitude of the studio managements toward their employees—her husband had been beaten up in the course of a peaceful demonstration outside the Burbank studios when Warner Brothers staged a lockout. By my English standards the views of my three friends were simply right-minded and liberal, but in the Hollywood of the time they were way out to the left.

This was the period when Senator McCarthy's witch-hunt was building to a climax. Hollywood was a prime target, with the writers and directors, as communicators, the most exposed. As far as I could see, any writer voicing the mildest democratic sentiments was likely to be arraigned as a dangerous communist. I remember, on a Sunday excursion with Silvia Richards to Lake Arrowhead, having some talk with Dalton Trumbo, top of McCarthy's "Hollywood Ten" most dedicated "commies." He was an excellent scriptwriter and most moderate in his opinions—though McCarthy's contention was, of course, that the conspirators worked underground and inserted subversive propaganda into their scripts. It was certainly not apparent in films like *A Guy Named Joe*, *Thirty Seconds over Tokyo*, or *Our Vines Have Tender Grapes*, which he had written; and it was inconceivable that authoritarian producers like the Warner brothers or Darryl Zanuck could have the wool pulled over their eyes.

The McCarthy hearings split Hollywood, with "super patriots" like Mrs. Leila Rogers (mother of Ginger), Adolphe Menjou, and Leo McCarey supporting them and forming a Motion Picture Alliance for the Preservation of American Ideals, and others like Katharine Hepburn speaking out against the smear and raising funds for the defense of friends whose lives and livelihood were being ruined. The studio bosses, for reasons of expediency, kept their heads down and discouraged stars, directors, and writers from engaging in "politics."

I recall a meeting called in defense of the Ten at the Beverly Hills Hotel, where, to the disgust of the downright Silvia Richards, Walter Wanger pointedly refrained from speaking in their favor but on the way out silently patted one of them on the shoulder. There was not much that I could do as a guest and a foreigner, but on returning to New York I gave Alistair Cooke a blow-by-blow account, which he used for one of his "Letters from America." Fritz was as indignant as the others, and I sat down with him to compose for *Theater Arts* an article that made his feelings on the subject clear enough.

The Los Angeles summer was now at its height, and it was breathlessly hot during the day. In the seclusion of our air-conditioned bungalow we would peruse the *Examiner* and the *Los Angeles Times* for the latest developments in the affair of the Hollywood Ten; the other burning topic was the running war in the Palestine protectorate between the occupying British forces and the Jewish insurgents. Here I found myself in a minority of one, decrying the murder of British Tommies while the others deplored the clashes on the beaches and the turning away of boatloads of Jewish immigrants from Eastern Europe. Meanwhile letters from home incongruously reported the worst winter within living memory, with roads blocked by snow well into April.

Through lack of funds I had perforce given up my comfortable quarters in the Beverly House Hotel and had found a room with a couple of kind-hearted Presbyterian schoolmistresses who had retired to California from Minnesota. They lived in an old timber house in Old Hollywood north of Sunset Boulevard, with a small garden almost entirely occupied by a large orange tree. It was at least considerably nearer to Universal City, and my routine was to breakfast at a drugstore on the boulevard (not the famous Schwab's, the haunt of out-of-work actors and extras, which was at the other end of the Strip) and then to take the now-long-departed Pacific Electric Railway across the Cahuenga Pass to a stop near the studio. It was, in fact, little more than a rattling old tram but useful nonetheless as about the only form of public transport in a city swamped by automobiles.

My existence was now one of extraordinary contrasts between the days, when I would be invited to eat at Larue or Chasens with Fritz and the others, and evenings, when I was reduced to buying myself a hamburger. Even at night the house never cooled down; linen from the chest of drawers came warm, as if from an airing cupboard, and the oranges from the tree in the garden were sun warmed.

By now a first cut of *Secret Beyond the Door* had been made, and it was decided to "sneak it" so as to obtain audience reaction. It was slipped in at a movie house in West Los Angeles—but with searchlights sweeping the sky, banners proclaiming a major studio preview, and a flurry of executive cars; a crowd of bobby-sockers with autograph books at the ready milled around the theater. There was polite applause, but the reception of the film was subdued; it was not one of Fritz Lang's best pictures, and it seemed to me that Michael Redgrave looked somewhat sheepish throughout, as if unconvinced by the twists and turns of the ingenious but unlikely plot. However, as is usual on such occasions when a great deal of money has been sunk in a picture, the brass decided that there was nothing that could not be put right by polishing and recutting.

My fellowship was now coming to an end. Fritz asked me to stay on for another year and Kenneth Macgowan of the Department of Theater Arts was keen for me to give lectures on English documentary at UCLA, but in the event the U.S. Immigration Service refused to extend my visa. I remember two acts of kindness on Fritz's part before I left Hollywood: his sending me to the best dentist in the place to cope with an emergency; and, when he heard that the funds from my fellowship were running out and that I planned to return to New York by Greyhound bus, his arranging for a sleeper on the Southern Pacific.

After my return to an England still suffering from wartime austerity, I kept in touch with him by letter and even interested him in directing a film for Gainsborough Pictures. By this time I was scenario editor at the studio and sent him the script of *So Long at the Fair,* a mystery story set against the background of the Great Exhibition in Paris. He was intrigued, and we offered him the picture—but could not, unfortunately, match his Hollywood fees. I never saw him again in person.

Fritz Lang was one of the cinema's outstanding directors, yet the publication in 1998 of a long and well-researched biography by Patrick McGilligan has produced not a considered assessment of such films as *Metropolis, M, Fury, The Woman in the Window,* and *The Big Heat* but a field day for uninformed and salacious reviewers. Why is it, incidentally, that even the quality papers have books reviewed by people who are largely ignorant of the subject? As Benny Green remarked appositely of a biography of Louis Armstrong, its reviewers, without any knowledge of music or jazz, completely misassessed his musical development and instead dwelled on his toilet habits and early experience of New Orleans whorehouses.

In Lang's case they took their cue from the subtitle of McGilligan's book, *The Nature of the Beast,* and latched on to a catchpenny phrase in the publisher's blurb—"The Monster with the Monocle." It was with disbelief that I saw the man who was (to me, at least, and our small team at Diana) so unfailingly civilized and considerate portrayed as a beast by an Oxford academic, branded with "pyromania, sadism, chronic mendacity and even murder," and further accused of modeling himself on Hitler and the "political gangsters"—who had in fact caused him to flee Nazi Germany.

Nothing is too trivial for reviewers who never knew him to use as a stick with which to beat him. His monocle makes poor Fritz a Prussian or a Nazi—but other talented German directors who worked in Hollywood, like Erich von Stroheim, also effected a monocle. (Fritz usually wore glasses, keeping his monocle for public appearances—and, for heaven's sake, he *was* in showbiz.) When it came to imperious behavior on set, it would be hard to upstage Otto Preminger. In any case, the last word in authoritarianism came not from Germany but from Nebraska— in the person of the autocratic Darryl Zanuck, who symbolically strode the lot at Fox Hills whip in hand, in riding breeches, long boots, and Tyrolean hat and instilled the fear of God into his producers, so much so that one of the most talented, my friend Kenneth Macgowan, quit for a professorship at UCLA.

I do not, of course, pretend to know all, or even many, of the answers about so complex a person as Fritz Lang, whose genius for suspense and the macabre clearly lay in temperament and makeup. However, I feel that I am speaking for others who can no longer do so, like Sylvia Sidney, Kenneth Macgowan, Joan Bennett (despite her tiffs with him), Arthur Kennedy, Silvia Richards, Lily Latté, and the many others who knew him well and shared my respect, regard, and affection for him.

A tiny reminiscence from my friend, the director Pat Jackson, seems to me to say a great deal about the man:

> I so agree with you about Fritz Lang. He was charming to me as a new boy in Hollywood. I met him at some cocktail party. I remember his saying and warning me: "Darlink boy, if one in ten of your assignments is one you half want to make, you are doing well. If you can't accept that you must go to another country, if you have another to go to."

Fritz's parting present to me was a collection of his favorite comic strips by George Herriman, *Krazy Kat*. In what e. e. cummings describes as "a meteoric burlesk [sic] melodrama, born of the adage *love will find a way*," the aggressive brick-throwing Ignatz mouse, for all the efforts of Offissa Pup, is constantly assaulting the gentle Krazy Kat. "Dog hates mouse and worships 'cat,' mouse despises 'cat' and hates dog, 'cat' hates no one and loves mouse."

No doubt, critics and detractors would identify Lang with Ignatz mouse and find in this further confirmation of his sadism. I prefer to remember what he wrote on the flyleaf:

> Dear Jan May you acquire Krazy's philosophy that makes a brick on his—(her?)—noggin the purveyor of true love. For the Krazys of this world there are *no* "austerities."
> Sept 29th—47
> Fritz Lang

CHAPTER SIX

The Polish Corridor

A few weeks after my return from the United States in October 1947—this time not on a Liberty ship but in style, on the SS *America*—I found myself installed in a small paneled and book-lined office at Lime Grove Studios, once occupied by one of the Ostrer brothers.

Many of the British film studios were named after trees and woods, like ours, Elstree, and "the wood called Boreham," as Orson Welles playing of a bemused continental producer in *The V.I.Ps.*, referred to M-G-M's former British bastion, but only Pinewood lived up to its name. Lime Grove was no scented avenue but a narrow thoroughfare connecting the bustling Goldhawk Road with Uxbridge Road and lying back from Shepherd's Bush Green. The studio, an improbable white building in modernistic 1930s style, faced the Hammersmith Baths and was wedged between Lime Grove and the tracks of the Metropolitan Railway. On the site of the old Gaumont studios dating from 1915, it had been constructed by the Ostrer brothers, like no other studio I know, with the sound stages one above another. It had been the headquarters of the Gaumont-British Picture Corporation at one of those bullish times when the British film industry was seen as the emergent rival of Hollywood ("It's good and it's British—it's Gaumont-British"), but by 1947 Gaumont-British and its studio had long since fallen into the maw of the J. Arthur Rank Organisation.

Starting in a modest way by making religious films, Rank, a Yorkshire flour miller and devout nonconformist, had embarked on a crusade for putting British films on the map worldwide. JARO had by then absorbed the Gaumont-British and Odeon cinema circuits and more or less every other major studio in the country—Denham, Pinewood, Lime Grove, Ealing, Islington, Riverside, and the rest—with the exception of Shepperton, Elstree, and Boreham Wood.

Our corner of this empire was Gainsborough Pictures (1928) Ltd., which took its name from a company founded by Michael Balcon and operated from a disused power station in Islington. The Gainsborough Lady, with her wide feathered hat, perhaps remains the most famous logo of British films—when we began making movies in color I had her redesigned by my cousin Michael Cummings, cartoonist of the *Daily Express*—but Sir Michael Balcon (or Micky, as he was known to film people) had long moved on to Ealing to produce the famous comedies and other pictures, for one of which I was myself to provide the story.

During the late 1940s Gainsborough had its own very definite role within the Rank Organisation. In 1947 the eighteen million pounds earned by American films in the United Kingdom accounted for a sizable proportion of the dollar drain from a Britain stripped of her assets during the war. On August 8, 1947, the Labour chancellor, Hugh Dalton, resorted to shock tactics and summarily slapped a huge 75 percent *ad valorem* duty on American films, and to add insult to injury he stipulated that the duty must be paid in advance on estimated earnings. The immediate response of the American industry was to embargo the export of *all* its films into Britain.

In a letter written to me at the time Fritz Lang spelled out what the film tax meant to Hollywood in human terms:

> When you in England think about Hollywood, I can imagine that you dream of a golden city of studios, nightclubs, swimming pools and endless sunshine. Probably, as you are unhappily forced to tighten your belts, you think the protest of the Hollywood producers over the new film tax exaggerated and lacking in feeling. . . . May I, as a working creator of films, who never owned a private swimming pool or made a Technicolor musical try to explain what your tax means to an ordinary citizen of Hollywood? I do this with all humility, because, like anyone who reads the

daily newspapers, I realize that a country that is fighting for its life and that must marshal its resources to provide its people with the very essentials of life, must rate entertainment a low priority. Is this all there is to the question? Your tax has had an immediate repercussion here. I would perhaps phone a friend in the studio production department—an unfamiliar voice at the other end. My friend had gone. It was the same at the prop department or the paint shop. And so it came as no surprise a day or two later, when I learned that one studio alone had sacked 500 people. They were mostly little people—50-dollar-a-week guys—and as you can imagine they felt bitter, bitter against England. Perhaps other methods of economy were possible—I'm sure that with time and thought other and fairer economies *can* be effected—but that's little consolation to a man who's lost his job and turns to a newspaper headline "British Film Tax" for explanation.

The government had in fact gone too far and landed Rank and the other British producers with the almost impossible task of replacing all the American films and making enough of the homegrown product to avoid blank screens or endless reruns in the cinemas. To do this Rank had to overstretch himself financially, borrowing heavily from the exhibition side of the business, and a couple of years later when the unworkable tax was abruptly withdrawn and the country was flooded with a backlog of American films, redundancies and closures of British studios matched those in Hollywood—as I was myself to find.

As far as Rank was concerned the expensive prestige product, such as the Olivier Shakespeare films, pictures like David Lean's *Oliver Twist*, the Launder and Gilliat comedy-thrillers, or set pieces like Michael Powell's *Black Narcissus* or *Red Shoes* were made at Pinewood or Denham. We at Gainsborough were set the task of making some dozen or more medium-budget pictures a year. They were certainly not quota quickies—they included some very worthwhile films like the Somerset Maugham *Quartet* and *Trio*—but the requirement was to release three pictures in as many months. Two pictures would be shooting concurrently at Lime Grove and one at Islington.

The wizard chosen by Mr. Rank and his chief lieutenant, John Davis, to balance quantity, quality, and budget was Sydney Box. In her entry in the 1966 *International Motion Picture Almanac*, Sydney's "little sister" Betty, who was to run Islington studios on his behalf, claimed that between them they had produced two hundred propaganda films in World War II. The Box family was therefore no stranger to jamming out the product, but what undoubtedly gained Sydney Box the job at Gainsborough was the runaway success of *The Seventh Veil*, an extraordinary mixture of psychiatry and Tchaikovsky that made not only his name but those of James Mason and Ann Todd.

Sydney Box was a big man in every sense. To begin with, he looked like Humpty-Dumpty and walked with a slightly rolling gait, aided by a stick. Cyril Hughs Hartmann, our historical expert on pictures like *The Wicked Lady* and *Christopher Columbus*, once wittily remarked to me that Sydney had a face like a swimming pool, but a swimming pool in which all sorts of interesting things were going on. He had his detractors, and saddled as he was with the schedule at Gainsborough, it was only too easy to criticize him as commercial and superficial. In fact, he knew just what he was doing and was lively minded and alert to a degree. An accomplished writer himself—he was responsible for some of the best scripts for the Maugham pictures—he was always on the lookout for new and inventive writers, and at one time or another I explored projects with Dylan Thomas, Christopher Fry, and James Forsyth. Sydney could charm a bird off a tree; he was usually willing to have a go (though he did, much to his later chagrin, pass up on my own *Blue Lamp*); another of his inestimable virtues as a film producer was that he made up his mind definitely and quickly and stuck to his decisions once made. In films, any clear-cut decision is sometimes better than vacillation and the right decision too long delayed.

As luck had it, when I arrived in London my good fairy, in the shape of Colonel Jock Lawrence, was already there to look over the new Rank product, including Olivier's *Hamlet* and rough cuts of new Gainsborough pictures. He asked me if I would like to go down with him to the projection theater at Lime Grove to see them and there took the opportunity to introduce me to Sydney Box, giving him, I am afraid, a somewhat exaggerated notion of what I had done with Louis de Rochemont and Fritz Lang. Sydney, always willing to take a chance, at once asked what I was doing and suggested meeting next morning, when, there and then, he offered me a job in the scenario department.

Those were the days when major studios, in England as well as Hollywood, maintained script departments with writers on contract, some of whom worked at the studio and kept office hours. Today, when vastly fewer movies are made, a producer will engage a freelance writer to work on a one-off project, but at Gainsborough, where a new picture was going into production every month or so, this would have been entirely impracticable. It was essential to have a backlog of finished and viable scripts—if only because there could be major problems over casting—so there were always some couple of dozen in the works. The progress of each, from the purchase of the original "property" through the various stages on the way to finished screenplay and production schedule, was recorded on a large board in the scenario department.

Like Sydney Box's elegant oval room, painted in shocking pink, and the other executive offices, the scenario department was on the Polish Corridor, so called because the Ostrer brothers, who had financed Gaumont-British and the building of the studio, were of Polish origin. The small but luxurious book-lined room that I was first assigned was just across the Corridor from the scenario department proper. It had, I think, been occupied by Bert Ostrer during his stint as a producer at Gaumont-British, and on looking at some of the handsome leather-bound volumes behind the executive desk I soon found that they were dummies and camouflaged a capacious cocktail cabinet, unfortunately empty.

The Rape of the Books

The real bookshelves in that first office of mine at Gainsborough housed books and scripts that I found intensely interesting. They comprised copies of the hundreds of properties acquired by Gaumont-British and Gainsborough or read in the scenario department with a view to acquisition, ranging from *Biggles* to J. B. Priestley's *Good Companions*, Somerset Maugham's *Ashenden* and short stories, or John Buchan's *Thirty-nine Steps*. There were also scripts, among them such classics as *Rome Express*, *The Wicked Lady*, Hitchcock's *The Lady Vanishes*, and those of the exhilarating musicals made, when Michael Balcon was head of production, by the captivating Jessie Matthews, of the endless legs and trilling voice—*Evergreen*, *First a Girl*, *It's Love Again*, and the others. (Later, in a disused basement, I came across a cache of all the original designs for Jessie Matthews's costumes. When Rank abruptly closed the studio in 1949, I tried to arrange for their handover to the British Film Institute or the Victoria and Albert Museum, but what happened in the general debacle, I do not know.)

Among the many reference books, two that particularly interested me were *The American Thesaurus of Slang* (how many of my predecessors had used it to beef up the unconvincing dialogue written for the American characters in British films of the time?) and *The Thirty-eight Dramatic Situations* by a Hungarian dramatist, who, after prolonged study, had reduced the basic situations of all films and plays to that number. They were firmly stamped "This is the property of THE SCENARIO DEPARTMENT Gainsborough Pictures (1928) Ltd.," but I confess to purloining both of them on the collapse of the studio, together with a battered stapler, still in use.

I grew attached to, not to say possessive about, the scenario department library, and when in due course I acquired an assistant I set him to work on cataloguing and arranging the books and scripts. After weeks of work Michael eventually got them into apple pie order. He was proud of his efforts, and Sydney Box lumbered down the corridor to admire the results.

Very shortly after this, Michael burst white-faced into my new office across the corridor. "They've come to take the books," he stammered.

"Take the books?" I said disbelievingly. "Who?"

"The props department."

"I'll soon see to that," and I jumped up and crossed to the library to find a couple of burly props with trolleys already beginning to denude the shelves.

"Now hang on," I said. "You can't do that."

"For *Quartet*," one of them said. "To dress the set. Mr. Darnborough's instructions."

I told them to lay off and hurried down the corridor to Anthony Darnborough's office—he was producing the picture.

"Look, Tony," I said, "what's all this about carting off our library. We've just spent weeks arranging it."

"Sorry, old boy," he said apologetically. "The Master's arriving in person in half an hour. He's recording the intro—you know, book-lined library and all that."

"But not *our* books," I protested. "Props should have ordered them. Sotherans hire them by the yard, classy, leather-bound books."

"They forgot," he said. "And the crew's standing by."

"Nobody ordered wolves," I remarked bitterly, and as there was nothing more I could do—production takes precedence of everything else in film studios—I went up to the sound stage and looked on as Maugham delivered his piece in front of *Biggles*, *The Thirty-eight Dramatic Situations*, and the rest of our jumbled treasures.

The head of the scenario department when I arrived on the scene was Sydney's wife, Muriel, who had started in the film industry as a script girl on the first picture ever made by Anthony Asquith and gone on to collaborate with Sydney on numerous scripts, notably *The Seventh Veil*. She was friendly, if a bit detached and possibly puzzled by my sudden appearance, since she already had an assistant in the shape of Peter Rogers (who was later to marry Sydney's sister Betty and to produce the *Carry On* films—Boxes within Boxes, as Cyril Hartmann once quipped about the ramifications of the Box family) and was in any case up to the eyes in rewrites.

Sydney, however, had not forgotten about me, and novels in proof, scripts, ideas written in longhand from people who thought they "would make a wonderful film" began arriving from his office down the corridor with terse requests for précis and opinions on them (nothing, in fact, that arrived at Gainsborough was ever left unacknowledged or unread—publishers and TV companies please note!). I was also sent theater tickets by the dozen to attend and report on plays, most of them productions that he had shrewdly decided to skip as unwatchable.

I was not left long on my own. Peter Rogers was soon promoted to associate producer, together with Tony Darnborough, Frank Bundy, Ralph Keene, and the others, and moved into an office of his own across the corridor; I then took over his desk in the scenario department proper, next to Muriel's. Much of my time continued to be taken up with preparing reports for Sydney, but Muriel increasingly involved me in rewriting and working on scripts. I also began supervising the freelancers who wrote the bulk of our scripts and negotiating terms with their agents (this was, in fact, how I acquired my own agent, Margery Vosper, having decided that she was among the shrewdest and fairest, and a lady into the bargain—there were agents so grasping that it was a penance to do business with them).

Muriel treated me at times as if I was at school, and at others like a mother; she had her own and very decided views about scripts; nothing, for example, that I could say in praise of Dylan Thomas's *Beach of Falesa* reconciled her to it. There was a great deal of lively to-ing and fro-ing between our desks, and I remember how when Somerset Maugham's *Quartet* was already on the floor we cast about for a final payoff line to the last scene of *The Facts of Life*, a story about the involvement of a young English tennis player with an expensive Riviera tart. Between us, we came up with "It could never have happened to a cricketer"—a line that one of the highbrow critics later hailed as encapsulating the whole story and being the "quintessence of Maugham."

Whether or not Sydney and she were grooming me for the part from the beginning, Muriel soon decided that she was more interested in directing films than in running a script department. Within a surprisingly short time, and still a relative amateur at script writing, I therefore moved desks again to the telephone-strewn monster beneath the great progress chart that ruled our existence. The final responsibility for buying or not buying books or plays and for approving prices and scripting fees was Sydney's. I was there to ensure, as far as I could, their smooth progression toward screenplays and shooting scripts. Sometimes, as with the Dylan Thomas subjects (never in fact to be made at Gainsborough), a producer and director were involved from the beginning; in other cases, like *The Blue Lamp,* for which no taker could be found among Gainsborough's producers, the screenplay was evolved entirely by the writer and scenario department.

We also serviced the scripts for the films produced by Betty Box at Islington. She was in charge of making the popular Hugget family series, starring Jack Warner, Kathleen Harrison, Susan Shaw, Dinah Sheridan (who left it to marry John Davis), Jimmy Hanley, and Petula Clark, even at the tender age of twelve a good singer and regular trouper. Many of the scripts were written by Ted (later Lord) Willis, but this was in itself such a big operation that the Boxes felt that extra help was needed in the scenario department, and so I was joined by Alan MacKinnon, a gifted thriller writer who had collaborated on two hit films with Roger MacDougall, *This Man Is News* and *This Man in Paris*.

Alan was vastly more experienced than I, with a mind like quicksilver and an instant answer to any scripting problem. The trio was completed by Gerry Bryant, who was later to direct Tommy Steele's first picture and whose forte was for revue and light and witty dialogue; he was taken on as a contract writer.

The three of us rapidly became fast friends and adjourned every lunchtime to eat and to drink pints of beer at the Shepherd's Bush Hotel, a vast Victorian pub almost as grandiose as the Shepherd's Bush Empire next to it on the Green, or at the British Prince in Goldhawk Road, a cramped and cheerful place much frequented by the technical staff (the food in the studio canteen was awful beyond words). In summer we used to walk over to the Doves in Hammersmith, next to the famous private press, and lunch on a balcony overlooking the Thames. Gerry was a confirmed punter, and at some point during the lunch hour he would always get a message to his bookmaker, who had assigned him the code name "Old Brocade," which he used when telephoning.

Critics have sometimes written about (or dismissed) the films we made at the time as "typical Gainsborough," but I find it difficult to identify any common element in the twenty or so we put out during my stint at the studio. There was, it is true, a tendency to make pictures about working-class people in contemporary settings, stemming from Sydney Box's earlier days in documentary—though these have sometimes been described as "patronizing" and not going deep enough. Such were the Hugget family films—a forerunner of television series like *EastEnders*—or *Holiday Camp* and *A Boy, a Girl and a Bike*, a story about a Yorkshire cycling club, one of Honor Blackman's first films, much of it shot on location in Halifax by Ralph Smart, fresh from Australia and *The Overlanders* and *Bush Christmas*.

I remember going up to Halifax to sort out some problem on the script and coming on Diana Dors in the writing room of the hotel, usually frequented by commercial travelers, where she was solemnly answering her first fan mail in longhand. She solicited my help. I liked her and wrote the part of Diana in *The Blue Lamp* for her (for some reason I never fathomed, Ealing cast it differently). I was much involved with Ralph and his producer Ralph Keene over the projected Dylan Thomas films; we later wrote three original screenplays together; and later still he became king of the filmed television series, producing *Danger Man* and others for Lew Grade.

Not all of my excursions from the studio were to places as unromantic as Halifax, and I remember one in particular to the French Riviera, my first postwar visit to the continent—the travel allowance was still only twenty-five pounds—in search of locations for filming. My companions were the director and the cameraman, whom I shall call George Rice and Leonard Harris.

Local Color

Leonard Harris was not the usual flamboyant cameraman. He was restrained and shy and displayed little trace of artistic temperament, apart from his uncanny ability to light a close-up or line up a pictorial shot. He normally dressed in an unobtrusive pepper-and-salt suit, and his ties were likewise unobtrusive. But, in spite of appearances, there was a deep stream of romanticism in Harris, which was of course why he had engaged in the hurly-burly of the film industry in the first place. His imaginative camera work was an escape from the humdrum of married existence, but there comes a time when artistic expression is not enough and a man craves the warmth and excitement of life.

We were booked into a hotel in Nice, and after a day spent along the corniche and up and down the coast we would forgather in the restaurant. Like other English visitors we soon discovered that, in an expensive hotel where a mere portion of melon costs twenty-five francs and our pounds were worth nine, our money went nowhere at all. We were often reduced to a diet of omelettes and *bière*. So it was that we spent less time eating than in watching the cabaret, or, to be more accurate, Giselle—for Giselle *was* the cabaret.

She was one of those singers who rely more on figure than voice—though this was pleasant enough in its husky way—and she was only too ready to vouchsafe the information that her waist measured thirty-six centimeters, no more and no less. Her tumbled mass of coppery hair and other attractions require no further explanations. When in due course she wandered among the tables, settling from time to time to take a glass of champagne, she deployed a frank and spawny look calculated (quite temporarily) to make any self-respecting male resent the presence of any other man within kilometers.

George and I soon sized her up for what she was, a tough little Parisienne, entirely aware of herself and determined to make the most of it, but the effect on Harris was catastrophic. Giselle quite mischievously played him up, gravitating more and more frequently to our table and settling on him from beneath centimeter-long eyelashes her long, cool glances.

In his inexperience, he was completely bowled over and waited until he was alone with George to ask his advice as a man of the world. As tactfully as possible George Rice indicated the strength of the competition, pointing out that there were well-heeled Germans and Swiss at the hotel who could afford to pay handsomely (in deutsche marks and francs) for Giselle's favors. Harris was disconcerted and upset. However, he was by now so far swept away that it was not long before he returned to the subject, reiterating that he was sure Rice was mistaken about Giselle and asking if he could make some discreet inquiries.

This was the easiest thing in the world in a Riviera hotel. Rice got hold of the headwaiter. He was himself taken aback by the size of the sum mentioned and got the man to write it down in new francs so that there could be no mistake. It made nonsense of Harris's modest expense allowance. However, in the face of Harris's gloom, we agreed to pool our resources. By the time Harris had cashed in all his traveler's checks he was in a position to get a message to Giselle via the headwaiter—he was too shy to approach her directly. And there was a new and inquiring look on her face the following evening; Harris, instead of taking his usual lager on the terrace, said an abrupt good night, blushed crimson, and disappeared.

Apparently he had it all laid on in his room—the bottle of Krug in the ice bucket, the dimmed lights, soft music from the radio. At long last, when he was preparing to call it a day, a tap on the door. He offered her one drink after another and meanwhile in pigeon French became more and more tangled in commonplaces about the beautiful weather, his work, and his wife. The carefully prepared envelope practically burned in his pocket. He was too embarrassed to make even a single move; even Giselle's composure deserted her in the face of his shyness. In the end, in complete nervous exhaustion, he pushed the envelope at her, stammered out some nonsense and bundled her out of the room.

Next day Harris blurted out that he had made a complete mess of it and promised to refund us in London. George remarked pointedly that he felt that *someone* should benefit from our sacrifices. But Giselle was left in a quandary and was not a little piqued. To do her justice, she came of thrifty peasant stock and liked to give value for money. She wavered between indignation and surprise until eventually she decided that Harris was the only real gentleman she had met in all her life. She knocked again the following night and for the rest of our stay would not look at another man.

As Rice remarked, it all goes to show that there are more ways than one of picking up local color.

Ken Annakin, like Ralph Smart, was another director whom Sydney Box plucked from documentary, but Sydney did not believe in typecasting and assigned him to that amusing comedy *Miranda*, in which Glynis Johns, with the aid of a flowing flaxen wig and a long tail made by the Dunlop rubber company, played the part of a sex-starved mermaid, ably abetted by Margaret Rutherford and Googie Withers.

Most of the directorial talent at the studio—Ken Annakin, Ralph Smart, Arthur Crabtree, and Harold French—took a hand in the two Maugham films, *Quartet* and *Trio* (a third, *Encore*, was later made at Pinewood after the closure of Lime Grove studios). Critically, they were perhaps the best received of our offerings, since the stories were straightforwardly and neatly scripted using the original dialogue wherever possible and cast with a galaxy of talent, including Dirk Bogarde, Jean Simmons, Michael Hordern, Nigel Patrick, Naunton Wayne, Wilfred Hyde-White, Françoise Rosay, George Cole, Nora Swinburn, Hermione Badderley, Cecil Parker, and Mai Zetterling, to name only some of the performers.

Dirk Bogarde and Jean Simmons also played opposite one another in *So Long at the Fair*. This subject—and I think that the film, which is sometimes run on television, still stands up—was one of my favorites. It was based on Anthony Thorne's novel and that intriguing mystery story about an English visitor to the Great Paris Exhibition of 1889 who disappears from a room of which the hotel denies the very existence. I spent a great deal of time over this script with the writer Hugh Mills, who gave it a lot of atmosphere, complemented by some really excellent sets.

It seemed to me that the story had the sinister and mysterious undertones that would make it an ideal subject for my mentor Fritz Lang.

With Sydney's approval, I sent him a script. He was keen to direct it, but unfortunately his agents named a figure way beyond our budget. In the upshot it was competently and briskly directed by Terence Fisher, whom Sydney promoted from the cutting rooms, but if Fritz had worked over the script and directed it, it would no doubt have been given an entirely different dimension.

Another title on that great progress board above my desk greatly intrigued me. It was *Scarlet Ladies and a Black Box*, but as other commercial middle-of-the-road pictures—*Broken Journey, My Brother's Keeper*, Edgar Wallace's *The Calendar, Portrait from Life* (for which Mai Zetterling first came to England), and the rest—were duly scripted and reached the floor, *Scarlet Ladies* remained obstinately stuck. I never could lay hands on a script, so it remains just a title, with infinite possibilities.

Historical epics were not the Boxes' forte, which was a pity, because the two films with the highest budgets and longest schedules were *The Bad Lord Byron* and *Christopher Columbus*. *Byron* suffered from a heavenly court and from being presented in flashback, and there were too many hands in the scripting. Muriel Box tried valiantly to pull it together, but it was not helped by lines such as "Oh, George, don't drink now, you should be writing." It was played by an embarrassed Dennis Price, with quite lively help from Joan Greenwood as Lady Caroline Lamb and Mai Zetterling as Teresa Guiccioli. *Columbus* was an expensive and ill-fated attempt to break into the U.S. market, and with this in view Fredric March and his wife Florence Eldridge were brought over from Hollywood to play Columbus and Queen Isabella of Spain. The script was slow paced and the dialogue inadequate, and what should have been a spectacular sequence on the high seas was ruined by the accidental loss from fire of one of the expensively constructed galleons.

Perhaps of more potential interest than any of the films that reached the studio floor was a group that remained on paper in the scenario department, notably two screenplays and an unfinished treatment for a musical by Dylan Thomas.

Dylan and the Last of Gainsborough

The extent of Dylan Thomas's work as a scriptwriter for films is not generally known. He was always something of a *cineaste* and first became professionally involved during the war, when he wrote commentaries for a number of documentary films produced by Donald Taylor at Strand Films—the company that had given me my first job in Cornwall. It was for Taylor that he wrote his only entirely original screenplay, *The Doctor and the Devils*. This script about Burke and Hare, the Edinburgh body snatchers, has been published in book form but was never filmed, because of objections from the censor. He worked on two further films, *No Room at the Inn* and *Three Weird Sisters*, before signing with Gainsborough Pictures.

The idea of signing him at Gainsborough came from Ralph Keene, well known for his documentary films and recently recruited by Sydney Box as an associate producer. Keene relates that a rival studio was also interested and that Sydney, having made up his mind over dinner one evening, forthwith got into his car, drove down to Brighton, and there and then reached agreement with Thomas to write three scripts over the following year. Under this contract he scripted *Rebecca's Daughters*, a historical piece about hooded raiders from Wales; Robert Louis Stevenson's *The Beach of Falesa*; and the fragment of a film operetta *Me and My Bike*, all in 1948.

It was the director Ralph Smart, an enthusiast for location filming and fresh from his work in Australia, who suggested adapting *The Beach of Falesa*. Dylan Thomas was an obvious choice for scripting it, since he too was a fervent admirer of Stevenson and had read almost everything that he ever wrote.

Thomas went to earth in the caravan near Oxford, where he was then working, and the script thereafter appeared by installments and in longhand. As scenario editor it was my task to keep an eye on progress, and this was anything but easy. His habit was to spend every penny of any advance before beginning work, and there would be desperate messages, begging for further advances to pay the tradesmen or buy Christmas presents for the children, so that scripting could continue. Writers ourselves in the scenario department, we did our best for him, but he remained the wonder and despair of the studio accountants. When he did get down to the script he wrote at great speed; there is a story, probably apocryphal, that months behind on a previous project, he had asked to be locked into a hotel bedroom with a case of whisky and finished both the script and the whiskey over a weekend.

As a person, I found him charming and without side or pretensions. He was unpunctual, it is true, to the extent of turning up for a script meeting a day or two late—generally with some such disarming excuse as that he had only a few minutes ago phoned his agent to inquire about the date. When he did arrive at Lime Grove it was always in a rumpled blue serge suit, looking like a merchant seaman on shore leave. There was never much work done on those occasions; instead, we inevitably adjourned to the Shepherd's Bush Hotel to drink pints of beer and listen to his Welsh stories, which he told beautifully.

A film script is a specialized literary form, and Dylan was not the man to bother overmuch with technical requirements. The prospective producer and director of *Beach of Falesa*—the two Ralphs, Keene and Smart—and we in the scenario department felt that with the first draft we had a potentially outstanding film on our hands, vivid, poetic, and marvellously eloquent. Muriel Box felt that there were weaknesses in the story and that it was unworkmanlike. Sydney, while agreeing that we should develop the script with Dylan, was curiously noncommittal. As I realized later, he was probably aware at that point that John Davis was about to pull the rug from under Gainsborough Pictures and that there was not a hope in hell of mounting an expensive location picture in the South Seas. I spent long and pleasurable hours, both at the studio and my flat, trying to iron out the story with Dylan, but most of the points agreed in discussion he used to forget in Soho pubs long before returning to Oxford and work. The final plan was that Ralph Smart and I should map out for him on paper the changes in construction needed for the purposes of filming and that he should see to the dialogue. Unfortunately, the sands were running out at Lime Grove.

Constantine FitzGibbon, in his *Life of Dylan Thomas*, dismisses *Beach of Falesa* as "obvious hackwork." It seems difficult to believe that he ever saw it or had the remotest idea of the extent of Dylan's enthusiasm for Stevenson and this story in particular. Here is a page, typed by my secretary from Dylan's holograph manuscript and dated October 7, 1948, describing the arrival of Wiltshire, the cockney trader, at Falesa:

THE SCHOONER. CAPTAIN'S CABIN.
  Wiltshire and the Captain sit at a small duty table laid with glasses and a bottle of gin.

CAPTAIN: Who's going to be mother?

Wiltshire half fills the glasses. We see him and the Captain CLOSE, the bottle between them. Wiltshire is a broad, dark-haired man in the middle thirties, stubbled about his strong jaw, shadowed under his eyes by dissipation or fatigue. He has a reckless twist to his mouth, but his eyes are contemplative: a man accustomed to some brutality and much loneliness, to excess and remorse. He looks into his glass, moving it slowly. A ship's clock tocks on the cabin wall behind him.

The Captain, bald and small and ageless, benignly wrinkled, deeply tanned and sea blown, an old salt soak, soft-mannered rogue and prop of all the Pacific bars, gossip of the Islands, raises his glass.

CAPTAIN: You've got the best little trading station I ever seen . . . (he drinks) All shipshape and Bristol . . . Clean as a skipper's cabin . . .

He darts a sly look round the cabin.

CAPTAIN: Maybe cleaner . . . Snug as a pub in the snow, trim and homey, three rooms all spit and polished, you could drink off the floor . . . When Johnny Adams saw it—Johnny with the club foot, him that was here before you—he took and shook me by the hand—this one with the mermaid on it . . .

He makes the tattooed mermaid on the back of his hand belly-dance as he speaks.

CAPTAIN (contd.): "I've dropped into a soft thing here, Conrad," he says. "So you have," I says, "soft as fevvers."

The Captain looks at Wiltshire's glass.

CAPTAIN (contd.): Your breakfast's getting cold . . . I only saw him once after that . . . Coughing and weeping . . . Gibbering when it grew dark . . . Peeping and sneaking and spying through the window chinks when the night comes on . . . Squealing in his sleep, like pigs . . . He couldn't get on with the natives or the whites or something . . . He carried a gun day and night but he couldn't have shot a whale, his fingers twitched like this . . .

He reaches to the bottle, refills the glasses. Wiltshire rises, huge in the little cabin, stares through the portholes. We MOVE UP behind him and look, with him, at the rapidly nearing Island, woods, trees, mountains, beach, the sounding surf, houses and natives on the beach.

CAPTAIN'S VOICE (over): Next time we came round he was gone. Vamoosed. Took a chance passage in a ship from up west. Case saw him off.

After the closure of Gainsborough in 1949 and in the removal to Pinewood Studios the file copies of the script were lost; there matters rested for some ten years. Fortunately, I had foreseen what was likely to happen and had retained my working copy. In 1958, with the good offices of Sydney Box, I was able to negotiate the sale of the script from the Rank Organisation to Israel Berman of Viking Films of New York, for whom I prepared a revised script incorporating the changes agreed with Dylan Thomas. The idea was to produce the picture, with Trevor Howard, Richard Burton, and Elizabeth Taylor playing the leads. I showed the script to Trevor Howard, who was keen about it, and on this basis both the Rank Organisation and later Sir Michael Balcon offered to put up the major part of the finance; unfortunately, Berman was unable to raise the balance in the United States. He eventually arranged for Dylan's script to be published in book form and later sold a controlling interest in it to Richard Burton. It would probably have made the best film of all Dylan's scripts, but there, sadly, the matter rests.

Like *Falesa*, *Me and My Bike* never reached the screen, and the file copies of the treatment were again lost in the transfer to Pinewood. Again, I had taken the precaution of keeping one, and it was thus that I was able to give it to Sydney Box, who, with the permission of the Rank Organisation, had it privately printed in 1965, donating the proceeds to the Screen Writers' Benevolent Fund. In his foreword to the book, Sydney describes the bubbling enthusiasm with which Dylan broached the project:

> *Me and My Bike* was never finished. It was scarcely even begun. As always with Dylan, it started with high hopes. His head appeared around my door, like a dissolute cherub's, his eyes shining with excitement. "I want to write the first film operetta," he told me. "It will be all about a man who loves a bicycle. It's called *Me and My Bike* and it covers the whole span of this man's life. He rides penny-farthings, tandems, tricycles, racing bikes—and when he dies in the end, he rides on his bike up a sunbeam straight to heaven, where he is greeted by heavenly choir of bicycle bells." Naturally I commissioned Dylan to write it. There were to be five major sequences in the film, each advancing the story through another decade. The fragment published here for the first time is only the first of the five, but is complete in itself—or would be if Dylan had ever finished it. The last page of the manuscript consists only of his working notes for the remaining scenes. After the shuttlecock and battledore

scene, he merely outlined the chase scene—and then disappeared. . . . *Me and My Bike* was written during the autumn of 1948 when Dylan was on contract to Gainsborough Pictures, of which company I was at that time Executive Producer. The typescript bears the date "2nd November, 1948." Of the other scripts written by Dylan during this period, *The Beach of Falesa* has already been published and another, *Rebecca's Daughters*, will appear shortly. Together they form the main volume of the work of Dylan Thomas, Screenwriter.

An extract from the script will convey the sense of fun with which it was written and belies the statement in Constantine FitzGibbon's biography that by this time his film work was "a mere job" and done "simply for money." This was certainly not my own impression, and after all, I spent a lot of time with him on these projects, both at the studio and at my flat in Wellington Square.

> Augustus on his penny-farthing is coming up the drive. We see his head above the bushes as he bicycles along in a hubbub of dogs barking and chickens squawking. Georgina is racing down the great stairs, her skirts billowing. She runs through the hall and opens the front door. On the steps, she stands to welcome Augustus. Augustus's head is bobbing up and down above the bushes of the drive. And now we see him, penny-farthing and all, ride up to the steps. A loud crowd of dogs barks, bays, bellows about the wheels. He wobbles. He alights. He raises his bicycling cap, and bows, stiffly and creakingly to Georgina. He stands at his penny-farthing's side, while Georgina exclaims in delight.
> Augustus!
> Georgina!
> And the two lovers burst into a kind of song, half operatic and recitative.
>
> | Georgina | How stern you appear |
> | | With your penny-farthen, |
> | | Augustus my dear, |
> | | So imposing astride it |
> | | And not scared a bit |
> | | Oh, I'd have a fit |
> | | If I even tried it! |
> | Augustus | For you I would ride it, |
> | | Georgina my dear, |
> | | From here to Carmarthen.

Georgina	Oh how brave you are then
	On your penny-farthen!
Augustus	Though it is, I admit,
	Very sharp where you sit.
Georgina	How impressively you pedal!
Augustus	How excessively it shakes!
Georgina	Your monster made of metal
Augustus	And every whisker aches.
Georgina	How aggressively you pedal!
Augustus	Though it hasn't any brakes.
Georgina	How handsome my love
(turns from Augustus	Upon his boneshaker!
and addresses the	How high up above!
audience)	How the winds reel behind!
	But the day I get on it
	I'll eat my best bonnet
	And the small wheel behind.
Augustus	Oh for a steel behind!
	Then I would take her
	From here to Jamaica.
Georgina	Oh he'd never take her
	Upon his boneshaker.
Augustus	Bicycles rot 'em, yes!
	Hell is not bottomless!
Georgina	How swivelly
	You are then
Augustus	Oh my liverly
	And lights
Georgina	On your nasty penny-farthen
Augustus	Where the saddle sits and bites
Georgina	How busily
Augustus	How dizzily
Georgina	How knobbily
Augustus	How hobbily
Georgina	You wobble and you sway
Augustus	O speedily
Georgina	Indeedily
Both	Take the brute away!

The Blue Lamp

Another subject never to be graced upon the screen by the Gainsborough Lady was of more personal concern to me; it was *The Blue Lamp*.

Sydney Box had inserted into my contract with Gainsborough a clause to the effect that, each year, I should write and give the studio first refusal of an original film treatment. I was still very much under the influence of Louis de Rochemont and felt that I should like to write something in semidocumentary style to be shot largely on location. Casting around for ideas, it came to me that a close family friend was Sir Harold Scott, commissioner of police for the metropolis. He had gone to school in Somerset with my father, and we had often as children watched cricket at Taunton with the Scott family (later I arranged for his daughter, Daphne, then working for her FRCP (Fellow of the Royal College of Physicians), to work as technical adviser on my first Pinewood picture for Rank, a hospital epic called *White Corridors*).

Thrillers involving the police were a stock in trade of the film business, but there had never been a picture depicting detective work on a sober, factual basis or portraying the life of a copper on the beat. Not at this point that I knew more than the next writer, but I asked Sir Harold if for the next few months I might spend my nights and spare time at police stations, on the beat, in squad cars, on police launches, or rounding up prostitutes at West End Central. He and his public relations officer, Percy Fearnley, at once realized what such a film might do in presenting a human image of the police to the public. (At that time there was no television and no BBC series like *Dixon of Dock Green*, a direct extension of *The Blue Lamp*, or *Z Cars*, which carried realism still farther. The first such series was, in fact, one that I myself wrote for the BBC, *Pilgrim Street*, based on Gerald Road police station and, ironically enough, shot at Lime Grove after the acquisition of the studio from Rank.)

Sydney Box jumped at the idea and gave it his immediate blessing, especially as we were promised the full cooperation of the Metropolitan Police, which no film company had achieved before. So I began my stint with the police, usually donning a raincoat, posing as a plainclothesman, and taking part in whatever action my current escort was involved in—which might be a precipitate call to the scene of a break-in, a pub brawl, the arrest of a prostitute, or simply a philosophic perambulation down the deserted London streets in the early hours.

My thoughts now turned to evolving a story, and Percy Fearnley gave me the files of a number of criminal cases. I was much struck by the Antiquis case, in which a jeweller was brutally murdered. However, I realized that with all the realistic trappings a murder case in itself was not enough on which to hang this film. I then hit on the idea of making my hero a copper on the beat, shot out of hand in a casual holdup at a cinema and so universally respected and loved that by all the rules he should have recovered in the last reel. The twist was to let Dixon die, so that every policeman at the station was emotionally involved in hunting down the murderer.

I duly finished a short treatment, prefacing it with the following:

September 21st 1948

THE BLUE LAMP
by JAN READ
(Revised Treatment)

N.B. The film has been written so that it can be shot among the streets and in the houses, shops and police stations of Greater London. Actual locations will very largely depend upon lighting, weather and other considerations. As I see it, the action will centre around Leman Street Police Station. The newer stations, such as Hammersmith, are lighter and more commodious, but lack atmosphere and associations. One has the feeling about Leman Street that its various rooms—the overcrowded office with its shiny Victorian furniture and shabby linoleum, the sanitary-tiled parade room, the winding gas-lit stairs, the policewomen's room with its rickety gas fire, the rabbit warren of a detectives office—have all been the setting for innumerable human tragedies. It will be much easier to get over a sense of comradeship in such crowded surroundings than in a concrete glass expanse. There will be plenty of opportunity to show modern police equipment at Scotland Yard itself.

I believe that a commentator can be a great help in knitting together a semidocumentary picture such as this, where real-life characters appear for a short space of time and are then lost. He should be a man who speaks with quiet authority and I wish to use him as was done in Louis de Rochemont's films, such as "BOOMERANG." In these pictures, the commentator, by mentioning definite street names and numbers etc., even though the names and numbers were invented, conveyed authentic atmosphere. . . .

Scotland Yard liked the treatment, and Sydney Box thought it a promising start; what it, of course, lacked was the dialogue to bring it to life. Not being a Londoner or brought up in the East End, I realized that I would have to bring in a writer who was or had been. As it happened, Sydney was about to go on vacation and had authorized me to spend up to a maximum of three hundred pounds on script work during his absence. It was not a princely sum (but, of course, worth more than ten times that amount today), and unscrupulously or not I decided to blow the lot on *The Blue Lamp*.

I was in no two minds about whom I wanted. Ted (later Lord) Willis was hardly the well-known figure he later became but a somewhat impecunious and underrated writer with just the background I was looking for, who had worked for us on the *Hugget* and other films. I showed him the treatment; he was agog at its possibilities and very shortly turned in a first screenplay, which brought the characters vividly to life and was everything I had hoped for. We worked over it together, and came the day when I confidently turned it in to Sydney Box.

His response was unexpected and downbeat. He did not like it himself, nor did Muriel or any of our associate producers, to whom, being an open-minded man, he gave it and asked whether they would be interested in producing it. But Ted and I refused to be discouraged; we were convinced that we had a winner. Ted, at least, had been paid his three-hundred pounds, but it then struck me that I had been paid nothing for my efforts over and above my regular monthly salary, so that the copyright belonged to me and not to Gainsborough. I taxed Sydney with this. He smilingly agreed, and when I went on to say that I should like to submit the script to Michael Balcon at Ealing, his immediate reaction was to pick up the phone, get on to Balcon, tell him that I had written one of the best scripts he had ever read (which for various reasons Gainsborough could not handle), and would he like to see me and it? This was shortly before Christmas. I saw Balcon, who liked the idea and subject, and said he would be in touch. I then took a train for Scotland and St. Andrews, to be greeted by a telegram reading: "WISH TO BUY BLUE LAMP IF PRICE REASONABLE—BALCON."

Of course I was enormously flattered that the prestigious Ealing Studios should want to buy the script. I agreed to the terms, and they quickly went to work on it, the shooting script being written by T. E. B. Clarke,

At the Armament Research Department, Sheffield. Jan Read, bottom left, holding shell filling. The milk was supposed to guard against fumes from molten explosive.

Jock Lawrence, inventor of Goldwynisms, with Sam Goldwyn. *Courtesy of Carlene Lawrence*

On location with Boomerang! in Stamford, Conn. Top: Center left to right: Boots Macracken, Dana Andrews, Elia Kazan. Far right: Louis de Rochemont. Bottom: Far left: Lee J. Cobb. *Courtesy of 20th Century–Fox*

Fritz Lang in his garden in the Hollywood Hills.

In Fritz Lang's garden left to right: Jan Read, Fritz Lang, and Lily Latté.

Mingote, cartoonist of the Madrid ABC.

At International House, NYC. Natalia Silva Bermúdez, self-appointed savior of the Venezuelan Theater.

Katharine Hepburn. "What, no big glorious head?" *Courtesy of RKO Radio Pictures*

Progress board in the scenario department at Gainsborough Pictures. Left to right: Jan Read, Eileen Griffiths (research), and Alan Mackinnon. *Courtesy of Gainsborough Pictures (1928) Ltd.*

In Noel Coward's words, "The Brontës of Shepherd's Bush": Muriel, Sydney, and Betty Box. *Courtesy of Muriel Box*

Muriel Box directing Eva Gabor in The Truth about Women. *Courtesy of Muriel Box*

Ava Gardner with Diana O'Brien and friend at the London Zoo. *Courtesy of Romulus Films*

Adrift during the Dutch flood disaster. Foreground left to right: Ed Hoornik and Jan Read.

Roger Furse, designer of many of Laurence Olivier's stage and film productions.

Nineteenth-century photograph of the King's Head and Eight Bells in Cheyne Row, Chelsea, gathering place for artists, writers, and show people. *Courtesy of Chelsea Public Library*

Maite Manjon, food and wine writer, married to Jan Read.

Jan Read.

himself an ex-police auxilary, and directed by Basil Dearden, much of it on location as I had envisaged. It proved to be one of Ealing's biggest successes and, because of its semidocumentary approach, fresh at the time, created an enormous stir. It was serialized in the *Evening Standard* and also triggered a long line of semidocumentary imitations.

On Ted Willis's advice, I had been sensible enough to reserve the dramatic rights in our script, and the first spin-off was a play, tried out at the Connaught Theatre in Worthing and then sold to Jack Hylton. In his production the tempo on variegated sets was maintained by using a large revolving stage, and the whole theater was utilized for the climax, the thugs being chased down the aisles of the auditorium. Some of the film cast, including Jack Warner, Robert Flemyng, and Patrick Doonan, appeared in it, and Warren Mitchell (much later to achieve fame in *Till Death Do Us Part*) played a brilliant series of cameos as the burglarized jeweler, a bent scrap dealer, and an Arthur English–style music hall performer, for whom he wrote his own patter. It still makes me laugh today:

> Clever stuff, this. Listen, I do my acrobatics next, I bend right over backwards and pick up a handkerchief in my teeth. For an encore, I bend over backwards and pick up my teeth.
>
> 'Ere listen, I just done fifteen days, no don't get me wrong—in the army—Z man that's me. I got to the unit—there was a sergeant, and what a lovely fellow, little black eyes and a yellow complexion, looked like a small portion of prunes and custard. He got us all on parade and he says: "You're all on manoeuvres this afternoon." He turned to me and said: "You camouflage yourself as a tree, get out in the enemy's front line and make observations." Half an hour later I was back. Sergeant said: "What are you doing 'ere?" I said: "Look, Sarge, I done like you said, I went out and disguised myself as a tree. I don't mind when a courting couple comes and leans against me, kissing and canoodling. I don't even mind when a dog comes along and mistakes me for a lamp post, but when a ruddy squirrel hops on, takes a peck at one of my eyeballs, shoves it up my jumper and says: "That'll do for the winter," I quit.

Warren's wife, Connie Wake, was also in the cast, taking over the part originally written for Diana Dors but played by Peggy Evans in the film.

The show broke all records for the 1952 summer season at the Tower Theatre in Blackpool and was then transferred to the London Hippodrome (later Talk of the Town). Here, it ran until about Christmas and then suffered an untimely end during the last of the great London fogs. There was no question of Ted coming in from Orpington to say goodbye to the cast; I found it difficult enough to grope my way across the road from Leicester Square tube station, and inside the theater the huge auditorium was more or less empty and full of fog. Wakes of this sort are sad enough in any circumstances, but on this occasion in the semi-murk, it was enough to make us all feel suicidal.

Despite the difficulty of the sets, *The Blue Lamp* was later performed in the provinces and, surprisingly, by amateur companies. Quite the most grotesque performance I remember was at the old Metropolitan music hall in Edgware Road, where most of the police seemed to be gay.

That, as far as I was concerned, was the end of the line, but Jack Warner was to play the part of a reincarnated Dixon, the murdered PC, in the long-running television series *Dixon of Dock Green*. This began with a handwritten note to me from Ted Willis:

> 4. 11. 54
> [November 4, 1954]
>
> Dear Jan—I may have the opportunity quite soon to do a TV series with Jack Warner.
>
> The idea is that he should play a policeman and I should like to use the actual names we created in the play—without encroaching on the film.
>
> If it comes to anything I should like to have your permission to do this. It is the names I'm after—the actual stories, of course, will be new ones.
>
> Yours ever,
> Ted

I gave permission, though I was a little puzzled as to how the names were to be separated from the characters—and this was not apparent in the series—but took no part in writing the scripts, which for twenty years were provided by Ted and his team. Apart from asking me whether I would prepare a radio version of our play in aid of the benevolent fund of the Screenwriters' Guild, which I did, he never—to my regret, because we had been very close—got in touch again. Ted did sterling work for the Guild and in helping to set up the Authors' Licensing and Copyright Association, for which he richly deserved his peerage, but it did seem hard that in making him a present of the television rights of *The Blue Lamp*, I lost a friend.

All this is looking a long way forward. By the time *The Blue Lamp* was premiered at the Leicester Square Odeon on January 19, 1950, I, like hundreds of others at Gainsborough, was out of a job. In the late spring of 1949 Sydney Box had mustered the entire staff on the largest of our soundstages and, on the point of tears, announced that Rank was summarily closing the studio. This was the result of the government's misconceived 75 percent *ad valorem* tax on American films and its subsequent abrupt abandonment, which allowed the whole Hollywood backlog to enter Britain in a flood. Rank had boosted his production to no avail, incurring a thirteen-million-pound overdraft with the National Provincial Bank in the process, and now only narrowly avoiding total suspension of film production.

Most of our people at Gainsborough went within a week; others on monthly salary remained briefly to clear up, until only the watchmen and the three-strong scenario department were left. There were several months of our contracts to work out, and we spent office hours each day during that long, hot summer in a room on the top floor above the soundstages, overlooking the whole of West London and the Thames. Alan MacKinnon and Gerry Bryant finished *Christmas with the Huggets* (which was never shot) and amused themselves by devising publicity slogans for *Kinematograph Weekly*—"Yule log a thousand laughs with *Christmas with the Huggets*." Tiring of this, after the daily ritual of solving the *Daily Telegraph* crossword puzzle Alan got down to his real love, writing a new thriller, while Gerry worked on lyrics, I think for *The Lyric Review*. I had been deputed to write a script of *Vanity Fair*, but as it was patent that nobody at Rank had the slightest interest in it, I got in touch with Eric Linklater, who gave me permission to script a book that had always amused me, his *Poet's Pub*, as a private venture.

Came the day when even our contracts ran out. We drowned our sorrows at the Shepherd's Bush Hotel, and Alan earnestly counseled me to go back to science if I still could. I should certainly have led a much more tranquil and prosperous existence if I had, but by now I had tasted blood in the film industry. I therefore continued with my script (but was pipped to the post when Rank bought the book and commissioned Diana Morgan to script it), working in my quiet Chelsea flat in Wellington Square, and waiting for telephone calls from film studios, which never came.

When an offer of work did come, it was unexpected and through one of my father's scientific colleagues. The 1951 Festival of Britain required someone with both scientific knowledge and experience in show business to help plan its scientific exhibitions on the South Bank. By now my finances were pretty strained; the job was a challenge and turned out to be interesting enough. The centerpiece of the Festival was the Dome of Discovery, later to be imitated so disastrously by the ill-fated Millennium Dome. Though in outward appearance they looked so similar, the Festival Dome was vastly more relevant to a country struggling to reorient itself and to recover from wartime austerities than were the vapid contents of the Millennium Dome to the Britain of 2000. Even Millennium Dome's ugly human figure seems to have been inspired—if that is the right word—by a tunnel in the Dome of Discovery (which I myself helped to design), in which one could walk, with increasing degrees of magnification, from the everyday world into the heart of an atom. But my heart was in films; I would get together with other refugees from Gainsborough, pester my agent to flog film treatments, and, when I was flush enough, take a girl to dinner at the Screenwriters Club in Deanery Street opposite the Dorchester Hotel.

Entertaining Miss Gardner

The Screenwriters Club (not to be confused with the Screenwriters Guild or Writers Guild, as it is now called) was at the time the most fashionable of meeting places for film people—not that many actual screenwriters could afford the prices.

There was a small bar on the ground floor and upstairs a restaurant with banquettes against the walls and about a dozen tables. The linen was spotless, the flower arrangements spectacular, and the food and wine excellent—I particularly remember a 1934 Gruaud-Larose, which was one of my favorites.

One of my dates was Catherine O'Brien, who had been Colonel Lawrence's assistant in London and was subsequently in charge of publicity on a series of large-scale Rank productions. Willowy, with striking black hair and an infectious, throaty laugh, she was one of the best publicists in the business. She hailed from Edinburgh, which apart from Jock Lawrence was a bond between us, and after a party at Lime Grove that we left together early after drinking more dry martinis than we should have, became more than friends.

It was after she had been on location with *Pandora and the Flying Dutchman*, which starred James Mason and Ava Gardner, that we had arranged to eat at the Screenwriters; at any rate, on this occasion she met me in the bar and asked if I would mind if we were joined by a friend who was on her own for the evening. I said by all means, and ten minutes later, in walks, dressed in slacks and sweater, the sultry Miss Gardner, who was staying over the road at the Dorchester.

She proved to be a lively and vivacious dinner companion, eating with a will and obviously approving of the Gruaud-Larose. She left early and asked if I would see her back to the Dorchester—by this time there was a largish crowd milling around the hotel.

I took her firmly by the arm and steered her toward the entrance, the teenagers meanwhile closing in around us and brandishing autograph books. We came to a halt, and she resignedly prepared to sign them. A cry now went up from the crowd: "Is Frankie there? Is Frankie there?" "No," she said firmly, "Mr. Sinatra is away tonight." At this, the teenagers melted into the darkness, leaving her stranded in the manner of that scene in *The Bandwagon* where Fred Astaire steps out of the train in New York and is surrounded by the press, only to be abandoned when *she* makes her appearance from the next carriage.

I felt a bit sorry for her, but she thanked me very charmingly, apologized for gate-crashing my date, and went in.

Altogether I spent four months in late 1949 and early 1950 at the Festival's office in Savoy Court, but by the time the great jamboree opened in 1951 I had long since departed.

It was at once evident from its reception by a packed audience of film people, the press, celebrities, and top brass from Scotland Yard and the Home Office, that *The Blue Lamp* was the British industry's biggest hit for years. I and my guest, a budding actress, were invited to dinner afterward at the Café de Paris by my director friend from Gainsborough, Ralph Smart, to celebrate with his wife (I do not think that it was on this occasion that I went to the Café de Paris with the Smarts to see Marlene Dietrich—that seems too good to be true!). However, even before the premiere I had been receiving tentative approaches from the Rank Organisation to rejoin the fold.

CHAPTER SEVEN

Doctors and Patients

My good fairy came in the unlikely guise of John Sullivan, a persuasive showbiz journalist, who had acquired an option on *Yeoman's Hospital*, a novel by Helen Ashton depicting twenty-four hours in the life of a provincial English hospital. She had for a time worked as a nurse and qualified as a doctor, and as in her *One Pair of Hands*, about a waitress, the book and characters rang true.

John Sullivan had obtained preliminary interest in making a film of the book from Earl St. John, the executive producer of the Rank Organisation, and needed a script. With my documentary leanings I was enthusiastic about the possibilities, and within days I was summoned to the Rank headquarters in South Street, Mayfair, and ushered into the presence. This, I thought, is where I came in. Like Spyros Skouras in New York, Earl sat at a massive desk situated on a low dais at the far end of an elegant and spacious salon. He was a big man with crinkly grayish hair, a boyish grin, and great charm, an exhibitor more than a filmmaker, and with rather simple and straightforward views on movies. As time went by I came to like him a lot.

The Blue Lamp was by now a smash hit, and I shared in the glory. He knew about my stint at Gainsborough from Sydney Box, and it now transpired that he wanted me not only to script *Yeoman's Hospital* but also to act as his personal story consultant at JARO—how true is the old showbiz adage that one is as good as one's last picture! We had a brief talk about the book, and he promised to get in touch with my agent about a contract. Earl was American, and he received regular and plaintive messages from Colonel Lawrence, 20th Century–Fox, and Universal that audiences in the United States simply did not understand half of what the characters said in British movies (nowadays the boot is on the other foot, with Hollywood actors eating their lines and making no effort to be understood outside Alabama). So it was that his last words at that first meeting, delivered in a deep Yankee drawl, were, "And, Jan, don't give me another of them English yappies."

Margery Vosper duly agreed to the terms for an annual contract with Rank according to which I was to write three scripts a year for what was for me an unheard-of amount, and I began work. I wanted to flesh out and update the story and began, as I had done on *The Blue Lamp,* with some on-the-spot research. I turned, oddly enough, to Daphne Scott, daughter of Sir Harold Scott, with whom I had been so involved over the police film. She and I had been undergraduates together at St. Andrews, and she was now studying for her FRCS (Fellow of the Royal College of Surgeons)—later she was engaged as technical adviser, given a room in which she could read her medical books at Pinewood, and was on call (in her scarlet St. Andrews gown) to advise the director and actors on the soundstages. In the first place she arranged for me to move into the North Middlesex Hospital as an intern, to accompany the doctors on their rounds of the wards, to sleep and eat there, and even (gritting my teeth) to watch in the operating room.

My idea was to extend and update the story by involving the young bacteriologist (played by James Donald) in work with radioactive isotopes. To plan his research and to get the detail right, I bethought myself of a former colleague from Sheffield University, Professor Wilson Smith—now, as luck would have it, head of the bacteriology department at King's College Hospital. Probably no hospital film was ever so carefully checked for authenticity, but even more important, of course, were the characters and keeping the story moving. My guiding principle—learned, I guess, from Fritz Lang—was that at the end of each scene the audience should be in suspense about what was going to happen in the next.

After much cogitation and contemplation of the tops of the plane trees in Wellington Square beneath my study, I produced a draft screenplay. John Sullivan liked it, as did Michael Balcon at Ealing, to whom it was sent for an opinion, and I was again summoned to South Street.

I should explain that the plot as rewritten centered on a small boy who developed a penicillin-resistant septicemia from an apparently innocent cut finger. By all the rules he should have recovered in the last reel; what generated the emotion was that (like Sergeant Dixon in *The Blue Lamp*) he died, and the young bacteriologist himself became infected through a graze from a syringe. This was later to cause ructions in the boardroom at JARO, when Rank asked in his downright Yorkshire voice: "Can't we 'ave a little 'ope?" However, for the time being all was plain sailing, with Earl commenting approvingly to me, "It's a situation pregnant with jeopardy."

John Sullivan was now in a position to make further plans, and we discussed the all-important question of a director; he came up with an idea that proved to be the making of the film—*White Corridors*, as I had rechristened it. Pat Jackson, a legendary name among the young British documentary directors, had been signed up by M-G-M on the strength of his wartime epic *Western Approaches* about the battle of the North Atlantic and, as John had somehow heard, was languishing in Hollywood. The proposal, in which I and, more importantly Earl, heartily concurred, was to send him the script and lure him back. It worked. Pat, as he told me later, had been left to kick his heels; out of desperation he had directed a couple of low-budget pictures for MGM and was only too anxious to come home. In the meantime I had reluctantly moved from my leafy top-floor flat in Wellington Square, off the King's Road in Chelsea—my charming landlady was remarrying and needed the whole house—to a mews cottage near the Embankment and Cheyne Walk. It ran to a spare room, and as Pat for the time being had nowhere to live, I suggested that he move in, so we could work on a shooting script together.

I had already with John's approval shown the script to my friend Maurice Carter, a modest but most talented art director whose work at Gainsborough on the Somerset Maugham films and others I much admired; he was now working for Rank at Pinewood. Maurice took to the project at once and drew up a plan for reconstructing the hospital across one of the main stages at Pinewood. With his drawings beside us, Pat and I now sat down and went through the script page by page, reviewing the dialogue, incorporating camera instructions, and adding new scenes and characters. Some were written for particular actors, as for Basil Radford, who found it impossible to be admitted for his back trouble, until he was unexpectedly knocked down and carried in on a stretcher. By the time we finished, we had a very good idea of whom we would ideally like to play the main parts, and the picture was later cast very much as we had envisaged, with Googie Withers, James Donald, Godfrey Tearle, Moira Lister, Jack Watling, Barry Jones, Mary Hinton, and, of course, Basil Radford taking leading roles.

The weeks went by very pleasantly. Pat was a fitness fan, and we often knocked off in the afternoons to play tennis on the Royal Hospital courts along the Embankment, sometimes with Jean Anderson and Helen Harvey, both of whom had cameo parts in the film (Helen, who was a sister of Frank Harvey, the playwright, later roped in her film director friends, the Boulting bothers). At midday we always walked along the Embankment to the King's Head and Eight Bells, at the bottom of Cheyne Row, for a pint or two of beer and lunch. It was through the pub that we discovered one of the central characters for the film and came close to casting another.

Sunday lunchtime was special at the King's Head and Eight Bells, with a crowd of a hundred or so forgathering from up and down town and overflowing into Cheyne Row and Embankment Gardens. One fine Sunday morning we spotted among the throng a slim and fresh-looking brunette and came to the simultaneous conclusion that this was our ingénue nurse to the life. To go up to her and offer her a screen test seemed likely to result in a slap in the face from her or the sturdy young man who was with her, but Pat was bolder than I and did just that. It turned out that she was, in fact, an actress; her test at Pinewood was so good that the decision, in the face of our enthusiasm, to cast Petula Clark instead was taken at boardroom level and for reasons of box office. In the event Pet, a child star of the *Hugget Family* at Gainsborough and now a renowned Parisian chanteuse, could hardly have done better in the part; I, at least, acquired a girlfriend and fell madly in love.

The film called for a small boy, and Pat, brought up in the documentary tradition, detested the cute kids provided by the casting agencies. Among my friends at the pub were a pleasant couple who lived in Shrewsbury House across the road, a businessman and his American wife with a son of the right age. Pat took to him on the spot, and he too was given a screen test. Brian Inglis was one of the hits of the picture, never on any occasion fluffing—he was nicknamed "one-take Inglis" by the crew. The taste of filmmaking decided him to embark on drama school and acting; he subsequently entered the antique trade and has recently appeared on screen as an expert on silver in the BBC's *Antiques Road Show*.

John Sullivan, who had worked so hard to set up the film, did not survive as its producer. JARO in its wisdom decided that someone with more experience was needed, and the project was assigned to the Italian-born Joseph Janni. I was personally sorry for John, with his warmth and enthusiasm, who after all had brought Pat and myself together and was now demoted to associate producer. (I was later to write another script for him, *Oh to Be in England*, about GIs and their amorous adventures in the United Kingdom. Sadly, he developed a brain tumor and died before the picture could be made.) Meanwhile, casting continued under the aegis of Joe Janni and the film was shot at Pinewood on schedule and without a hitch. I suppose that *White Corridors* came as near to a *film d'auteur* as is possible in Britain or the United States. As Pat wrote me recently, "Dear boy, we had the best of it. When I think of the complete freedom we had in the making of WC it's mind boggling. Now the vampires have the industry by the throat." Thankfully, Rank did not get his way with the story changes, and despite JARO's misgivings the picture ran and ran at the Leicester Square Theatre and was in fact one of the biggest grossers of 1951. My guest at the premiere was Sarn A'Deane—the girl who lost out on the screen test.

Ten years on, long after I had left the Rank Organisation and was freelancing, I was to write another medical film of a very different sort. *That Kind of Girl* was the brainchild of an unlikely couple—Tony Tenser, a film publicist turned producer, and Michael Klinger "an ex-striptease impresario," as the *Sunday Telegraph* described him at the time (later he produced some large-scale epics, such as *Zulu*). The idea was to make a story film about teenage VD, "a strong subject," as Tony claimed in his press releases, "but treated with taste." It cost fifty-thousand pounds (a reasonable budget, considering that a first feature with established stars cost around two-hundred-thousand pounds at the time and a B feature as little as fifteen thousand). Tony added, "We could have made it at half the price, and three times as dirty. But that's not the way to do it."

I was hauled in on the strength of *White Corridors* to supply the story—and, I guess, the taste! My solution was to put it to Tony that if he wanted to clear the film with the censor for distribution and to obtain cooperation from the medical profession he must obtain a seal of approval from the British Medical Association and display it on the credit titles. This was to prove my salvation and that of the film, because in the last resort I could always invoke Dr. Ernest Claxton, the formidable general secretary of the BMA, whom I involved from the beginning.

He was an ardent member of the Moral Rearmament Movement, and I remember accompanying him, to show that my heart was in the right place, to elevating shows like *The Crowning Experience* at the Westminster Theatre, then leased by the movement, and visiting the Brighton Boys' Club with him. In fact, we became quite good friends; we discussed my ideas for the script, and he gave me all the introductions to doctors, social workers, clinics, and hospitals that I could possibly need. I then began a round of interviews with specialists like Dr. King of the London Hospital in the East End, Dr. Nicol of St. Thomas's, and Dr. Dalziell-Ward of the Council of Health Education. At the other end of the scale I paid visits, sometimes incognito, to the discreet basement premises labeled "special clinics" of hospitals like St. George's. Somehow or other I managed to walk a tightrope between my unlikely sponsors and the medical world, and when Tony and I lunched with John Trevelyan of the British Board of Film Censors, he agreed to the script with only minor alterations.

The story, as I recall it, hinged on an au pair girl raped by a socialite cad and a suburban teenager entangled with one of the left-wing protesters objecting to the U.S. Air Force base at Aldermaston. It was cast with unknowns, and I wish that I could remember their names, because they turned in excellent performances. It was directed by a talented newcomer, Gerry O'Hara, who went on to make many more films. It was marketed as "The Shock Film of the Year," but a review in *Kinematograph Weekly* nevertheless described it as "compulsory viewing for adolescents," and oddly enough it proved especially popular with women. I myself was so impressed by its message that I subsequently arranged to have a VD test in Harley Street—happily negative!

By now I was beginning to feel at home in the medical world and had even, on some of my white-jacketed rounds of the wards, been addressed as doctor and asked for advice. My next foray began in July 1962, while *That Kind of Girl* was still in production, with a call to the BBC Television Centre. The connection it produced was to last on and off for three years.

I was summoned to meet Harry Green, script editor for a projected new series of thirty-nine fifty-minute episodes to be entitled *Alan Finlay M.D.* (later rechristened *Dr. Finlay's Casebook*). Harry was a Welshman, big in every sense, and one of the best editors I ever worked with—helpful in discussing a storyline, skillful in reworking or cutting a script, and an expert at the telling one-liner. At this first meeting he explained that the BBC had bought the rights to a short episodic novel of A. J. Cronin's entitled *Memoirs of a Black Bag*, about a country doctor in the Highlands of Scotland. There was enough story material in the book for about half a dozen scripts, after which it would be a question of inventing new stories revolving around the shrewd old Dr. Cameron of the novel and two new characters, the rather brash young Dr. Finlay and their housekeeper, Janet. The plan was for a small team—in the first place, as I remember, Harry, his gifted compatriot Elaine Morgan and myself—to write the scripts. He gave me the book and asked me to think about it.

I was interested on two scores: by now I was thoroughly acquainted with things medical and used to writing about them, and secondly, I had been brought up and gone to university in a small Scots town, where my GP and his patients mirrored Dr. Cameron and his. I therefore set to work with a will, drawing on two of Cronin's stories for my first script and introducing a new character of my own, Jamie Gibson, a lugubrious Tannochbrae undertaker, who proved so popular with audiences that he regularly reappeared in later scripts by other hands. The Cronin stories soon ran out, and I drew on a rich vein from the many highly individualistic St. Andreans, town and gown, whom I had known in my school and university days. (Some, indeed, especially the academics, were eccentric to a degree, like the eminent Professor Stout, author of the famous *Manual of Psychology*, who meeting my father in the street one day remarked to him, "A strange thing, Read, one of my legs seems longer than the other this morning." He was, in fact, walking with one foot on the pavement and the other in the gutter.)

The stories were set in the 1920s, when, of course, antibiotics were undreamed of. There were herbal-based remedies like digitalis, still administered as foxglove tea; the popular antiseptics were iodine and carbolic acid; chloroform and ether were in general use as anesthetics; but of modern synthetic drugs there were more or less none, other than aspirin and salvarsan (for treating syphilis). Drs. Cameron and Finlay therefore relied a great deal more than today on their own resources and skilled diagnosis, and in an emergency would carry out surgery such as a tracheotomy or appendectomy in a farmhouse bedroom (I myself as a small boy remember having my tonsils removed and also an eardrum perforated on a white-draped table in the drawing room—albeit by a specialist from Dundee). All of this led to more drama than the modern practice of referring anything serious to a hospital consultant.

My guide on matters medical was another friend from the King's Head and Eight Bells, Dr. John Vyse, son of the Chelsea potter Charles Vyse; he ran the Casualty Department at the Charing Cross Hospital. He had seen so many unusual cases that he was the ideal person to help work out the twists and turns and surprise ending of the typical *Finlay* plot—on occasion his wife, a West Indian nurse, also lent a hand. John was also well versed in history, medical and other, and steered me off anachronisms, knowing just what had been possible in the 1920s and what had not. When I had the glint of an idea, we therefore repaired to the King's Head or to his own local, the taproom of Fuller's brewery in Hammersmith, to kick it around. For example, *The Immortal Memory*, a story about Burns Night, was tied in with that of the president of the society, a local optician, who in proposing the toast kept misquoting from his notes and as it transpired was convinced that he was going blind. The solution was much simpler: he was a canary fancier, and the transparent husk from a seed had attached itself to his eye, giving rise to all the symptoms of his self-diagnosis of keratitis. This, of course, was based on a real-life case in the casualty ward.

John Vyse and I shared another interest, jazz. He was a friend of the brilliant trombonist and bandleader Chris Barber, to whom he introduced me, and on occasion we went to 100 Oxford Street to listen to Humphrey Lyttleton. We used, of course, to buy 78s from those collectors' bibles, the *Parlophone Rhythm Style* and *HMV Swing Music* catalogs, with their glossy 1920s-style photographs of stalwarts like Joe Venuti, Slim Gaillard, and Charlie ("Yardbird") Parker. It is often hard enough to devise titles for television episodes, and later on I found the indexes at the end of these *chefs d'oeuvres* of Edgar Jackson a goldmine—"Somebody Loses, Somebody Wins," which I used for an episode of *Man in a Suitcase,* was one of my favorites (I never heard the original, performed by a black vocal and instrumental trio, The Three Keys).

Once a backlog of scripts had been accumulated, rehearsals began. These took place in the unglamorous surroundings of church halls, boys' clubs, and the like, up and down west London. Writers were asked to attend so as to be on hand to make on-the-spot changes to the script where a scene did not work out as intended or the actors had difficulty with the lines. We had been asked to confine the action to some half-dozen small sets, and the studio material, recorded at the Television Centre in Wood Lane, was supplemented with location footage shot at and around Callander on the verge of the Trossachs, which did duty for Tannochbrae.

I soon became fast friends with the trio playing the lead parts—Andrew Cruikshank as the shrewd and experienced Dr. Cameron, Bill Simpson playing the more impetuous and thrusting Dr. Finlay, and Barbara Mullen, the supportive and perceptive housekeeper who kept the bachelor establishment afloat. I would say that the runaway success of the series owed more than anything to the humanity of the three and the "chemistry" between them.

Finlay was a tight ship in its early days; in the first place it was scheduled to run for thirteen fifty-minute episodes, but series after series was called for, and I contributed some dozen scripts to the first four. In all, around 160 episodes were produced. I felt that like most long-running series, it eventually began to show its age, and I even found that in the latter stages some of my stories for the early scripts had been "borrowed." Script editors, writers, and directors all changed—some of them, to my mind, displaying little knowledge or feeling for things Scots. What remained constant throughout was the faithful trio of

Cruikshank, Simpson, and Mullen. In the upshot the series did Bill Simpson little good. He was indelibly stamped as Dr. Finlay; he never played another worthwhile part and returned to Glasgow, where he drank more than he should have and, sadly, died young. Andrew, of course, was such a thoroughly good and human actor that he went from strength to strength.

CHAPTER EIGHT

At the King's Head and Eight Bells

When I first came back from the United States and landed a job with Gainsborough Pictures, the most pressing thing was to find somewhere to live, and an advertisement in the *New Statesman* caught my eye. It was for a furnished flat in Chelsea, comprising the top two floors of a house in Wellington Square. At that time, Chelsea was still the abode of artists and writers, and I always felt that once the number 19 or 22 bus had cleared Sloane Square and Peter Jones, one was entering another world. The atmosphere was almost village-like; the King's Road was still home to artists' colormen and frame makers, with streets of low houses disappearing toward the river; even the light seemed to have a quality of its own.

Wellington Square was small and gave off the King's Road, with a garden and plane trees in the middle, and number 24 was at the bottom, a four-story Regency house. The basement was occupied by Rupert Hart-Davis, the publisher, and the house belonged to his sister, who was in the throes of divorce. I liked her and decided on the spot that the top two floors, with their views into the square, were for me. They were not divided off from the rest of the house, and on occasion I felt a bit of an interloper when Deirdre was giving a party for her daughter and I had to plough through the couples sitting on the stairs, and even more so when once on my way out I knocked on the door of her sitting room and she advanced stark naked—I was evidently not the visitor she was expecting! However, in time I got to know her daughter Susie (and had some part in her going to St. Andrews University) and even began dating her very pretty and aristocratic friend, Jane—a job in films impressed young women.

I grew most attached to the low-ceilinged living room at the top, with an open fire for which in those forgotten days a long-suffering morning woman lugged up the coal, and in which I wrote at a table overlooking the tops of the plane trees. On weekends, in my guise as scenario editor, I sometimes invited writers for informal script meetings. There was a bank holiday session with Hugh Mills in which we hammered out the final storyline for *So Long at the Fair*. Arnold Ridley, who wrote *The Ghost Train* and later became one of the Stalwarts of *Dad's Army*, was another visitor. Other meetings at his club, the Savage, began with talk about scripting but ended up at the bar with Jimmy Gold of the Crazy Gang. I can still see Dylan Thomas puffing up all the stairs to my aerie on the top for one of our numerous sessions on *The Beach at Falesa*.

Adjoining the living room was a kitchenette, where my cousin Jean Cummings, sister of Michael Cummings, the *Daily Express* cartoonist, gave me my first cookery lesson—by instructing me in the art of boiling potatoes. I subsisted mainly on bacon and eggs, sausages and kippers, but when entertaining a girl the great standby was '"Frood," a precursor (made by Joe Lyons) of the modern fast foods.

As well as the bachelor fare, my guests would on occasion share my bed—this, after all, was the time of the swinging 1950s and 1960s in London. Nevertheless, a word of explanation seems needed at this point. I had left for the United States and Hollywood on a pink cloud, having weathered the short-lived and disastrous marriage to another man of the girl I had been in love with since university days and in the expectation that, all going well, we would marry when I returned. We had written regularly, and one of the first things I did on arriving in London was to see her. Yvonne then broke it to me that in my absence she had met and was shortly to marry a distinguished diplomat. He was the most charming man—to the extent, years later when they were on leave and invited us to lunch, of donning his full governor general's regalia with feathered cocked hat for the benefit of my Spanish wife. I found it difficult to envisage the somewhat dreamy Yvonne as a peeress arranging official banquets at distant residences, but so it turned out, and being the positive person she was, she made a great success of it. For me at the time, the bottom seemed to have fallen out of my life. All I could do was to put my best face on it and, quixotically enough, present the couple with a treasured Derain chalk drawing as a wedding present.

Such was the state of disillusionment in which I embarked on the first of my liaisons, with a woman rather older and certainly more experienced than myself—a lively, decorative, and elegant Russian on the point of separating from her husband. I think we had sized each other up and were both spoiling for sex. At any rate, after dinner at Wellington Square one night she parted with her Chanel top without demurring, and then I removed her bra to bare her splendid breasts. She lay on my bed and we talked amicably while she told me how she had once had TB and the chest I so much admired had been collapsed. At this point I undid her skirt and was about to take off her knickers, when she opened her eyes wide and unexpectedly blazed at me, "How dare you!" I dared, and after that it developed into the easiest, most undemanding of affairs—bruised as we both were, we were neither of us looking for long-term commitment.

She was as down-to-earth as Garbo in *Ninotchka* and simply took it for granted that when we were alone we would copulate. With half-moon eyes full of merriment, she would joyously unzip me and take possession. In retaliation I undressed her thoroughly and comprehensively, from her designer blouses to her high heels. Having had our way, I would lend her a dressing gown and make coffee, and we would talk in the relaxed and familiar way of the sexually contented. Sometimes she read my hand; what she predicted for me I forget—except that she never suggested that our relationship would continue. I think we were sensible enough to realize that we were destined to go our own ways.

She was a woman of metal, high-spirited, and with a flair for paintings and for cooking carp with ginger. On one occasion she asked if I would lend fifty pounds to a young French artist who had run out of cash in London. I did so, never expecting to see it back, but he insisted on giving me the address of his agent in Paris. Some time later, en route for Lisbon with the British naval attaché, Norman Todd, we were involved in a car crash in the Rue de la Paix. These were the postwar days of the thirty-pound travel allowance, and we had not the wherewithal to pay for the repairs or for staying over. At this juncture I thought of the young artist and betook myself to his agent. Blow me down, it turned out that the young man was now wildly fashionable; his agent paid over the money in francs and, more than that, arranged for us to stay at the economical Petit Auberge in Beaugency until the car was ready!

The bedroom at Wellington Square overlooked a house in Smith Street occupied by Robert Newton, the actor and ultimate Long John Silver, whose wild parties often kept me awake. A few doors down was an Indian restaurant (later prosecuted for serving dog food in its curries) patronized by Laurence Olivier and Vivien Leigh, who lived nearby. Also in Smith Street was the Phoene Arms, where I lunched on occasion in the dining room, with its rickety bentwood furniture and brown lincrusta walls. It was not the most cheerful of pubs, and I soon began faring farther afield to the King's Head and Eight Bells, the habitués of which were to play so large a part in my life.

I have always been a believer in pubs rather than clubs—the clientele are so much less predictable—and was a regular at various times of hostelries other than the King's Head. When we lived in Lowndes Square my wife and I used to go for a lunchtime pint to the Wilton Arms in Kinnerton Street. Tucked away in a narrow mews, it had no doubt been built to solace the coachmen and servants of the large houses in Belgrave and Lowndes Squares. We had often remarked on a reticent-looking man in dark coat and hat and slippers, who habitually sat by himself over his gin and tonic; one day John, the landlord, said that he would like to introduce us to a fellow writer. It turned out that he was none other than Henry Greene, author of some of the most individual of twentieth-century English novels; he lived around the corner. We became good friends, and our lunch breaks were enlivened with accounts of the *jeunesse dorée* of the thirties, in the style of *Party Going*, and his visits to France and Spain in a Proustian, chauffeur-driven Hispano-Suiza tourer. Recluse as he was, he even on occasion donned shoes and climbed the ninety-odd steps to our flat for dinner at Lowndes Square. Rather before that another favorite port of call was the Salisbury in St.

Martin's Lane, with its mirror glass and copper statuettes (originally designed, I believe, as electroliers). For me the Salisbury means Peter Finch, newly arrived from Australia, and assorted actors from *I Am a Camera*, particularly the girl for whom I so regularly waited until curtain time at the adjoining New Theatre (now the Albery), who understudied Dorothy Tutin and who in spite of Dottie's proverbial ill health never had a chance to go on. It was she who obtained free tickets from Donald Albery for *Waiting for Godot*. I was then writing scripts for John Larkin, the talented Hollywood scriptwriter and producer, for a television series, *Fabian of the Yard*. The performance was way above the heads of us Hollywood hacks (John had written scripts for my pinup girl, the siren-voiced Alice Faye), and we adjoined for the second act to the Salisbury, later meeting with Jocelyn at the adjoining Leicester Grill to retrieve the remains of the evening.

In the summer of 1950 I regretfully moved from Wellington Square—Deirdre Balfour was getting married again and needed her top two floors—to a mews cottage in Dilke Street just behind Cheyne Walk and the river, and close to Physic Garden of the Royal Society of Apothecaries and the Sitwells' house in Swan Walk. The cottage had at one time belonged to Lord Ivor Spencer Churchill, a great wine fancier who had installed a cellar and wine racks. It was at the time that I myself was beginning to take a serious interest in wine, and I proceeded to stock them, believe it or not, with 1929 Chateau Brane Cantenac and 1928 Chateau Margaux at twenty-six shillings (two dollars) a bottle, and, for everyday drinking, 1940 Chateau Ducru Beaucaillou from my friend Ronald Avery in Bristol. He let me have the Beaucaillou for nine shillings, since, having the space, I took twenty cases off him, peddling some to Chelsea friends, as it was more than even I could cope with.

Barring other engagements, I used to frequent the King's Head and Eight Bells, now my local, both for lunch and in the evening. The white stucco building stands picturesquely on the corner of Cheyne Row and Cheyne Walk, known for their associations with Carlyle, Ruskin, Swinburne, and the Pre-Raphaelites, and was separated from the Embankment and the Thames by a narrow garden. Inside, it was divided into a public bar with a wooden floor, a tiny "jug and bottle" (where customers brought their own receptacles to be filled and taken away), and a more comfortable saloon bar with an open fire in winter. Each had its own entrance, and the serving area was at the center, with etched glass panels (much admired by that *enfant terrible* of Chelsea artists, Augustus John) screening the saloon bar from the others. The one person to visit the "jug and bottle" was a distinguished-looking man in a velvet smoking jacket, who shuffled down from his house in Cheyne Row in carpet slippers to fill a silver-mounted tankard. He was, in fact, a prominent merchant banker, and his sons, who used the public bar, were the Ingrams brothers, founders of *Private Eye*.

Even then, the studios of Whistler and his peers, like those in Tite Street near me, with their great north-facing windows, were being bought up and converted into flats by the new meritocracy, but opposite the King's Head in Cheyne Row there was, and still remains, a group of low-built studios arranged around an internal patio. They were then occupied by Roger Furse, the designer of Olivier's plays and films; Charles Cundall, of the Royal Academy; and Charles Vyse, the potter. All were habitués of the hostelry opposite, but it was Charles Vyse who was its mainstay.

Charles, brought up in the potteries of Staffordshire, was one of the last of the studio potters, whose hand-thrown vases, bowls, and dishes were finished with glazes based on the ancient Chinese and compounded from wood and other ashes—one of his rich patrons used to provide cigar ash in quantity to make the classic grey-green Celadon. His pots commanded, and still do at auction, high prices. Then in his seventies, he still put in long hours at his wheel and kiln but spent his lunch break and the evenings at the pub, occupying the same corner and always in the same flat cap, loud-patterned jackets (reduced, as he explained, because no one else would buy them), beige cords, and brown suede shoes. He was never without his pipe and his pint; alert and outspoken, he was always stimulating and was on terms with almost everyone who walked into the saloon bar. He had an eye for a pretty girl and, having trained as a sculptor, would verbally undress any attractive new arrival for one's benefit, concluding that most were too skinny about the thighs to pose as artist's models. Skinny or not, he was soon offering them the perfumed snuff from silver boxes—there were two varieties, the "boy" and the "girl"—which he bought at an expensive tobacconist in the Haymarket. He was my guide and counselor as regards female form, offering his comments, sometimes outspoken, on the actresses and models I brought in from time to time.

Charles, who cooked large stews in his studio for himself, did not actually lunch at the pub. Instead, he sat in his corner next to those of us who did, at a solid, mahogany-topped table with cast-iron legs, to which, on occasion, I used to tether an Alsatian wished on me by an actress girlfriend on provincial tour—a hound that used to sleep on the end of my bed and watch me type film scripts. It was given to howling when it felt that it was time for the daily walk around Battersea Park, thus provoking peremptory rings at the door from animal-loving matrons who accused me of maltreating it. Its owner was the same Sarn A'Deane whom Pat Jackson and I had discovered at the pub, and for whom I had now fallen hook, line, and sinker. This high table was reserved for us few who forgathered every day and was presided over by Lady Vernon Brown, crippled with arthritis but a formidable and witty lady, extremely well read and an opera lover—and woe betide any interloper, who received such a look as to retire precipitately to the uncomfortable restaurant in the rear quarters.

Among those who joined us on occasion were Lady Brown's husband, the urbane Air Commodore Sir Vernon Brown, one of the survivors of the original Royal Flying Corps of the 1914 war and later Chief Inspector of Crashes for the Air Ministry; Father de Zulueta, the priest of St. Thomas More in Cheyne Row, a cousin of Cardinal de Zulueta, who died tragically in a bathing accident when in Jerez de la Frontera, where he was born; Roger and Ines Furse and an itinerant American, Joey Ramsdell, who had turned up at their house one day and years later, to Ines's irritation, was still staying with them. An embattled-looking individual with furrowed face and curly white hair, he designed sets at Covent Garden and helped Roger to make models and miniatures for his films. It was he who taught me in my bachelor days to make authentic corned beef hash.

On rare occasions Charles Vyse would himself sit down at our table to lunch and would then ceremoniously remove his cap—to reveal a bald and shiny head. There was little love lost between Charles and Lady Brown. She thought his talk of pots and glazes a bore, and he habitually referred to her as "Ma Brown." Charles had an assistant, Barbara Waller, a serious, dark-haired young woman and a talented sculptor in her own right. She did not often make an appearance at the pub, and Lady Brown insinuated that Charles was denying her any social life; she would invite her to opera and concerts, which did nothing to improve relations. Matters reached a climax when at lunch one day Lady Brown announced that her daughter "Bun," as she was nicknamed, had given birth to a son. "It's too easy," chortled Charles, riding a favorite hobby horse, "a sow could do better!" Fortunately, I was sitting between them.

The King's Head and Eight Bells was, I suppose, more than most pubs a place for meeting friends and making new acquaintances, and it had the edge on a club in that one never knew who might appear through the door, and on private sociabilities that one could depart at whim. That the door on occasion opened to admit Rex Harrison and Kay Kendall, Ingrid Bergman, or Marilyn Monroe may seem more surprising, but this was because they were the guests of the Furses across the street.

Roger Furse was a man of enormous charm and distinction, a gifted artist and perhaps the most famous of British production designers. He designed the settings for Laurence Olivier's plays and was responsible for the sets and costumes of a host of films, beginning with *Henry V* and including Hollywood epics like *Spartacus*. I had first met him when doing a story about the filming of *Richard III* at Denham Studios for *Hollywood Quarterly,* before becoming a near neighbor. Ines kept open house in Cheyne Row for visiting film people, whom Roger would often bring to the pub; I remember informal dinners at the long table in the basement of the studio where one might find oneself next to Claudette Colbert, Ingrid Bergman, Brigitte Bardot, Jean Seberg, Claire Bloom, or Marilyn Monroe (whose stormy joint venture with Olivier, *The Prince and the Showgirl,* was designed by Roger). Then there was Joan Castle, an American actress and friend of Roger from a stint in New York, who came to stay in London and married a scion of the Sitwell family. To everyone's surprise she became chatelaine of a huge unheated baronial pile in Northumberland, where Bill, who had been a commander in the Royal Navy, abandoned her for weeks at a time while he skippered a coal ship from Newcastle to London to raise money for maintaining the place. Later, he abandoned poor Joan altogether for her best friend.

Ines, outgoing and spontaneous, had been a seamstress in Paris when Roger first met her but was unabashed by her illustrious guests. Kay

Kendall, bidden for lunchtime drinks, once remarked in my hearing, "Ines dear, do you always hang out your laundry on Sundays?" Roger liked his whiskey and once declared to me, "This is a one-bottle house," meaning that the bottle was never left unfinished. I think we must all have imbibed a lot when one evening shortly after Maite and I were married Ines left the room after dinner and reappeared stark naked to perform a fan dance for us and then poured a tin of curry powder over my wife's unfortunate head. Maite has never cooked curry since and hinted darkly that Ines fancied me and that this was oblique revenge on her part—she could be pretty forthright in her behavior—for my own omission to do with her what I never could with my best friend's wife.

The largest gathering that I remember at the Furses' studio was the breakup party for *The Roman Spring of Mrs. Stone*, based on the novelette by Tennessee Williams and produced by Louis de Rochemont, who called me in to write additional dialogue. It was the only film on which I worked with Roger, who, because of a ban on location shooting in Rome after the furore caused by *La Dolce Vita*, constructed part of the Via Veneto across the largest stage at Elstree and together with Joey Ramsdell made a magnificent model of the Roman skyline as a backdrop to Mrs. Stone's balcony. It was Vivien Leigh's last picture, and a young Warren Beatty played opposite her. He was accompanied at the party by the glamorous Joan Collins, who watched jealously if he so much ventured to look elsewhere—at my startlingly beautiful Spanish wife, to begin with—and *she* had her work cut out to avoid the attentions of the charming and voluble writer of *Marty*, Paddy Chayevsky. It was in vain that she tried to escape to the loo, which gave directly off the main studio, with its drapes from *Henry V* and Roger's treasured Picasso drawings; he pursued her, voicing endearments through the open top and bottom of the door—few of which she understood, her English being limited at the time, and puzzled as she was by behavior so novel to a well-brought-up *madrileña*.

The Furses were among our best friends in London. Maite stayed with them before we were married, and I can still see Roger bearing a Hepplewhite chair, their wedding present to us, up the ninety-two steps of the flat in Lowndes Square to which I had recently moved. We could not immediately go on honeymoon, because I was in the throes of a script for Boris Karloff, with the usual deadline. When we did, Roger and Ines joined us for the first leg in France, for which I hired a car, and we drove in leisurely fashion down the Rhône Valley, stopping at places like Beaune and Pouligny to taste the wines and then continuing through Arles, Avignon, Aigues Mortes, and Narbonne to Collioure. Here we had a farewell lunch at La Balette, perched high above the sea, and Roger sketched us all before we headed over the border into Spain.

Memory, as Henry Greene once wrote, is like a country lane, in which with its high hedges and many twists and turnings one soon gets lost. I wish that I could recall more of the people I encountered at the King's Head. Mary Ure, briefly and unhappily married to the playwright John Osborne and an actress of great promise unfulfilled because of her premature death, lived nearby and occasionally joined us. There was Jocelyn James, who understudied Dorothy Tutin and with whom I was much smitten, and her French friend Kiki, outgoing and vivacious and a dream of a cook—now married to the Comte de Chiris of the famous Grasse fragrance house, and one of the few from that time with whom we are still in touch.

The talented and darkly handsome Sandy (Alexander) Mackendrick of Ealing Studios, later to direct *The Sweet Smell of Success* in Hollywood, was a bird of passage. Then there was the dashing David Livingstone-Learmouth, editor of *Horse and Hound*—or was it *British Racehorse?* Carnation in buttonhole, he always looked as if he had come straight from Ascot. Yet again, there was John Vyse, son of Charles Vyse the potter, and head of the Casualty Department at the Charing Cross Hospital, who helped me with stories for *Dr. Finlay's Casebook*. He brought in with him a Dr. Abrahams, a pioneer in investigating allergies, who, learning that I was subject to frequent catarrh, enlisted me as a guinea pig for his experiments at the Royal Naval Hospital in Greenwich and discovered that I was particularly sensitive to dust from Maltese donkeys!

I have left to the last perhaps the most important characters in the drama played out each day at the pub: Bertie Noble, the licensee, and her husband Bill. The King's Head and Eight Bells belonged to Whitbread, the large brewers. Most London pubs are now run by managers on behalf of the owners, but Bertie and Bill were tenants, responsible for their own finances and free to take their own decisions, thus making for much greater individuality. Bertie was a vivacious, attractive, and down-to-earth woman in her late thirties, while Bill, tall, burly, and dark, was surprisingly a customs officer—which did not prevent him from pulling pints in the evenings and on weekends. Bertie was somewhat laconic but was on Christian-name terms with her regulars, and when on occasion, to meet some script deadline, I found myself standing at an empty bar, marooned in London over the Easter or Christmas holidays, she could be unexpectedly warm and friendly. She ran the place meticulously, with gleamingly polished counter and tables, and an inviting linen table cloth and cutlery set out for lunch in the saloon bar. It was a shock for us all when one Sunday night, driving back from Brighton with her husband, they ran into a tree and she was killed outright.

My friend and mentor Fritz Lang told me that he had often thought of making a film about someone whose whole life was changed by slipping on a cherry stone; the nearest he came was in *Woman in the Window*. A chance encounter at pub can prove equally momentous, and the King's Head and Eight Bells exerted its alchemy on many of us who frequented it. As James Howell wrote long ago in the seventeenth century,

> This life at best is but an inn,
> And we the passengers

After my contract with Rank ran out, I embarked on the swings and roundabouts of freelance writing. Sydney Box, having lost *The Blue Lamp* to Ealing, now got in touch with me to write an original story about the women police, shrewdly realizing the value of my contacts with Scotland Yard. The project had its light side, as when I introduced him to Shirley Jennings, then a sergeant but later to become a Dame and head of the women police; he took us to dinner at Les Ambassadeurs, where he impishly tried (entirely without success) to ply her with more champagne than she could take. The film was directed by Muriel Box and, released as *Street Corner*, was quite a success.

Shortly after this I received a summons to Pinewood from my old boss Earl St. John, who asked me if I would be interested in writing a film about a flood disaster that had recently ravaged Holland. I duly set out for Amsterdam and was assigned as collaborator the Dutch poet and journalist Ed Hoornik. He and his wife, Miesje, who later became head of children's television in Holland, introduced me to the Amsterdam scene, including the Seewall, the famous red-light district, and the café, which unaccompanied males entered at the risk of being shorn of their ties. Later Ed and I toured the flooded polders, narrowly avoiding being swept out to sea in a rowboat. We toiled over a story and were later joined by an old master from Hollywood, Anthony Veiller, but in the upshot the film was never made.

The picture that I remember best from this period—if not entirely for cinematic reasons—was *Blood Orange*. Michael Carreras, whose Hammer Films specialized in horror movies with stars such as Christopher Lee, approached me about something in a rather different vein, a thriller about a fashion house. I liked the idea and rustled up introductions to some establishments like Hardy Amies and Worth, so as to learn something about *haute couture*. Having duly sat out a quota of fashion shows on the gilt chairs of the salons, visited the dressing rooms and workshops, and found a title for my film in the name of one of Hardy Amies's striking party dresses, I thought that I should like to find out more about the life of the models. With this somewhat risky object in view, I dated one or two of them—and, of course, became immediately involved.

One of the girls to whom I turned for advice was a friend of Sarn A'Deane, my King's Head discovery and whom I had known and liked for ages without paying any particular attention to her. In her early twenties, she always gave me the impression of having gone to Roedean; she had all the nice manners and inhibitions one acquires at a good girls' school. She modeled in the boutique of a fashionable Knightsbridge department store and was somewhat amused that I had got in touch with her but agreed to come to supper at Dilke Street and to chat about the rag trade—and this we did until supper was over. The conversation then became more personal, and I began to realize what an extremely pretty girl she was, in a dark, almost oriental way.

It emerged that she had long had an understanding with a childhood friend, now a tobacco planter in Kenya, and that she would in due course go out there to marry him. It all struck me as very much like Alice Faye in *The Stowaway*—minus Shirley Temple. However, a complication had arisen in the form of a foreign diplomat, married of course, with whom she had had a torrid affair and who had now cynically ditched her. I felt for her; there were tears in her eyes as she spoke about it, and one way or another she never went home that night but got into bed with me.

Over the next month or two I took her to restaurants and cinemas and occasionally to the cottage, but by tacit agreement we did not repeat what had taken place. However, like Henry Higgins in My Fair Lady, I was growing accustomed to her face and to her ways, and when she turned up for a premiere at the Leicester Square Odeon in a dress with an absurdly long train I would have ridiculed on anyone else, I marched two paces behind her to avoid its being trampled on and was proud of her to a degree.

A day or two later, she came round for dinner. As soon as she was in the sitting room, she faced me and launched out, "Jan, I have a great favor to ask"—and then, in her most ladylike voice, "will you please fuck me tonight?" She liked to do things in the proper order, so we had drinks, ate, listened to a little Duke Ellington, and she then got up and left the room. I waited and then went to look for her, and found her clothes neatly folded in approved boarding school fashion on the bathroom chair.

By now I was taken enough with her to march her straight to the nearest registry office, had she been willing, and as we lay together in the morning, I demanded from her whether she seriously intended to wed the Kenyan tobacco planter. She interrupted me and said in the nicest way, "Jan, please don't ask me." I think she was right. We really had not enough in common to live together. Had I any right to barge in and upset her long-standing plans? I thought not, and before long she departed for Kenya.

That was to be my last bachelor fling at Dilke Street. In the meantime I moved in with a friend from Reuters at his flat in Shrewsbury House, which was even nearer to my indispensable King's Head and Eight Bells, practically overlooking it.

CHAPTER NINE

The Spanish Connection

I do not know why I was so enamored of Spain, even before I had actually been there. Its "slow old tunes" and the excitement of flamenco, the agonized saints of El Greco and brocaded Velásquez beauties, the exploits of the conquistadors, Cervantes who "smiled Spain's chivalry away" and Lorca silenced in his prime, all caught and held my imagination. Spanish was the only foreign language that I taught myself for pleasure and is now the one that I speak and understand the best.

During the blackout and the dark days of the war, it was at Martinez Restaurant in Swallow Street, with its Andalusian patio and splendid *azulejos*, that I used to meet Oscar Oeser, who had long ago collaborated with me on the St. Leonard's film in St. Andrews. He was now a squadron leader in the RAF and working at the hush-hush decoding establishment at Bletchley Park—though this was something I was not supposed to know. Secretive as he was, I kept it a strict secret from him that I did know; my brother also worked at Station X, hence my inside knowledge. Later, when as scenario editor at Gainsborough I entertained writers to dinner, it was usually to Martinez that I invited them and treated them to paella, tortilla, or *zarzuela*.

Again, when my vivid Venezuelan friend from New York, Natalia, turned up in London and married her Free French pilot, it was there that I hosted their wedding breakfast. When I think about it, it was probably her dark looks, her Spanish ancestry, and outgoing Latin temperament—my first encounter with a flesh-and-blood señorita—that so attracted me to her.

In the years immediately following the war, with the tiny travel allowances, I never got nearer Spain itself than St. Jean Pied de Port in the French Pyrenees—which was at least Basque—and my first visit was arranged by Catherine O'Brien, who, as I have described, introduced me to Ava Gardner while looking after publicity on *Pandora and the Flying Dutchman*. In fact, Catherine had a habit of bobbing up at turning points in one's life: it was she who introduced me to Roger Furse; she rediscovered Natalia, now divorced from her French pilot and playing a small part in Olivier's *Richard III* in Spain, for which Catherine was doing publicity; and years later, after marrying Korda's publicity chief Bill Bachelor, she approached my wife about collaborating on a Spanish cookbook and started Maite on her career as a food writer.

In 1951, shooting on *White Corridors* had recently finished, and I was in need of a holiday. Catherine suggested Tossa de Mar, which she had got to know well during the filming of *Pandora,* and put me in touch with the man who had made the location arrangements, Rafael Toscano. Tossa, on the Costa Brava north of Barcelona, was then a small and picturesque fishing place with a curving beach surmounted by the ruins of a castle, narrow sandy streets, a few bars, two small hotels, and a few *residencias*. Rafael was the only travel agent, and he worked from home.

I asked my actress friend Sarn A'Deane if she would like to come. She had her reservations until I suggested that my cousin, Michael Cummings the cartoonist, would join us. Sarn and I had been seeing a great deal of each other, we were very good friends—but I suspected that there was perhaps someone else in the wings. I had several times been on holiday with Michael, but like me he had never been to Spain.

We duly flew to Barcelona and were met by Rafael, who was all Catherine had cracked him up to be, full of energy and enthusiasm. He installed us in the Solimar Hotel in Tossa and we began a pleasant enough holiday round, swimming and sunbathing, exploring the castle ruins, taking part in the ritual of towing the net out each morning and hauling it in to the beach teeming with small fish, and of drinking from a *porrón* in the fisherman's bar. Meanwhile, Rafael organized excursions. We went in a donkey cart to a deserted villa, where he cooked paella—not very expertly, so that when I hid my helping under a pile of leaves, it was embarrassingly excavated by the attendant dog. More ambitiously, he hired a car, an ancient Erskine and the only one available in Tossa, for visits to the market town of Santa Colona de Farners, where we lunched with a friend of his, and to Hostalric with its Napoleonic fortifications. The only snag about this was that the owner of the Erskine turned up with his arm in a splint; after he had come within inches of putting us over a precipice and it turned out that his arm was broken, I insisted on taking over and driving the old brute of a car with its primitive gearbox along the miles of fearsomely potholed roads.

We were at dinner one evening when someone produced an English newspaper. Sarn glanced at it, put down her knife and fork with a clatter, and burst into tears. In banner headlines was the news that a Royal Navy submarine had foundered in the Solent, and it now transpired that the young man I had on occasion met with Sarn was a lieutenant on board her. The following days were spent listening to the radio and in making telephone calls, but all the rescue attempts were in vain, and the whole crew of about a hundred was lost. I was next awakened one night to be told that Sarn had been found by fishermen wading into the sea; there was nothing for it but to cut the holiday short and return home. Rafael, whom I was to see on further visits to Tossa, had been so supportive that I shipped him a set of Linguaphone records for teaching the townspeople English—thus, I am afraid, helping to hasten the day when the village was to become the tourist resort that it is now.

My serious involvement with Spain began five years later in summer 1956, when I was asked to Sunday lunch by a journalist friend Sheila Gould, editor of *Modern Woman*. I had been invited, I guess, as her only acquaintance who could speak tolerable Spanish, to meet a young woman who was looking after her baby. Maite was slim and petite and wore absurdly high heels, and with her bright eyes and short curly hair she looked a bit like a mischievous boy. However, I soon discovered that she had studied medicine at Madrid University and was working as theater sister, a senior and highly trained nurse, with a distinguished surgeon at a specialist hospital in Santander; he had decided to send her to London to learn English so she could translate medical texts for him.

After lunch Sheila suggested that I take her to the cinema, which I duly did (to see John Mills in *The Way to the Stars*), and from there to the King's Head and Eight Bells, where Charles Vyse offered her the "boy" and the "girl" and looked her over appreciatively. From then on I used to spend evenings with her at St. George's Square while she was baby-sitting. I cannot say that her English improved a great deal, but we certainly fell for each other in no uncertain way, and came the day when she declared that she was returning to Spain to make arrangements for the wedding. There was no discussion—I had always been in love with the idea of marrying a Spanish girl and for the last few months particularly this one—and I simply suggested that it might be polite for me to write in such Spanish as I could muster to ask permission from her father.

In due course I had a guarded letter from him, but it was one thing for Maite to plan marriage with a Protestant in Spain and another for the Roman Catholic church to approve it. The weeks went by, and her letters became increasingly impatient, so that in the end I turned to my friend Father de Zulueta of St. Thomas More in Cheyne Row. He gave me some instruction and wrote to his cousin, the cardinal archbishop of Madrid, and it was finally agreed that we might be married at the Goya church of San Antonio de la Florida. Meanwhile, two or three months of stubborn opposition had roused all Maite's Spanish pride, and she now decided that she no longer wanted to be married in Spain but at a registry office in London. For her to depart unmarried to England not unnaturally alarmed her parents, and in the upshot I had to send her a one-way BEA ticket to Heathrow. The delay had at any rate given me time to move into a roomy flat—not, alas, in Chelsea but in Belgravia. She arrived on my birthday, November 18, and three days later a few friends, including Ines Furse, Charles Vyse, Michael Cummings and his wife, and a forgiving Sheila Gould, turned up at the Chelsea registry office to see us married (a year or so later, when our son was on the way, Father de Zulueta married us again in church, at St. Thomas More).

The flat, in which we were to live for almost thirty years, overlooked Lowndes Square and its plane trees at the front and the old Pantechnicon furniture repository at the rear. It was spacious, light, and airy—as well it might be, at the top of ninety-two stairs. The lack of an elevator posed few real problems, with a helpful porter and at a time when the man from Harrods would climb them all simply to deliver a loaf of bread. The steps were a different matter, however, for heavy smokers; we were concerned that our friend Les Norman, the Ealing director, might expire on the spot after surmounting them. Coming from a family in Madrid still surrounded by fleets of servants, my new Spanish wife knew nothing about housekeeping, and to begin with I did most of the cooking. However, I had a "treasure" of a cleaning lady who had followed me from Dilke Street to Shrewsbury House and now to Lowndes Square; she turned up every morning to tidy the flat and took Maite shopping, besides teaching her some basic cookery skills. We talked together in Spanish, and I despatched her to the Berlitz School in Oxford Street to learn English, for which she departed most mornings like an unwilling schoolgirl. Needless to say, I adored her, and she enchanted my friends—even my normally brusque doctor, Elizabeth Graham Kerr, who sent me a note that said simply, "I think your Spanish señorita is sweet."

Visits to her parents and to my own in Scotland—who were almost as apprehensive as hers about our sudden marriage—had to be postponed, because I was in the thick of a script for Boris Karloff. I had been introduced to its American producers, Richard Gordon and Chuck Vetter, by a Wardour Street stalwart, Nat Miller, for whom I had scripted a B feature, *The Secret Tent*. (The film was directed by Don Chaffey, with whom I later worked on *Jason and the Argonauts*, and beautifully played by a cast that included Andrée Melly and Jean Anderson; it turned out remarkably well.)

Dick and Chuck wanted an original story. I had recently read and been much struck by Walter de la Mare's dark novel *The Return*, and I evolved something along (what I hoped) were fairly sophisticated Jekyll and Hyde lines—at any rate Karloff very much liked the script, and it was shot by the up-and-coming Robert Day, later to go to Hollywood and marry Juliet Prowse. Released under the somewhat penny-dreadful title of *Grip of the Strangler*, it has, to my surprise, become part of the Karloff canon and something of a cult movie. Chuck wanted me to write a sequel to be called *Corridors of Blood*, a cheapjack title that

Boris loathed and I so much disliked that I refused to write the script. But Chuck had odd tastes. Rather later, we had him to dinner with his wife, and Maite cooked a paella. We were surprised to see him sorting out what was on his plate into neat piles; he explained, "I only eat what I can identify."

Boris and his poised and charming American wife, Evie, were living at the time in Cadogan Square very near us, and we became good friends, seeing a lot of each other. Belying his screen appearance, he was the most thoughtful and gentlemanly person. Like myself he was devoted to cricket and had umpired matches for the famous Hollywood club, and we shared an admiration for Conrad, of whose novels he had a complete edition at Cadogan Square. After his death, by which time Maite had become an accomplished cook, Evie would sometimes come round for a Spanish meal.

At the time, Lowndes Square was a little film colony. When we first arrived, the flat below us belonged to the vivacious copper-haired Adrienne Corri, who had a role in the notorious *A Clockwork Orange*. I had known her long before. She later moved to a house in St. John's Wood, where she threw Sunday parties for stage and film people, at one of which her small sons were discovered trying to sit our even smaller Carlos on a chamber pot. Her flat was then taken by Virginia McKenna and Bill Travers. Our neighbors across the landing were Sir Charles and Lady Evans. Charles had been commodore of the royal yacht and now headed the British Film Producers Association. His wife, Angèle, was Greek, highly temperamental, and given to quarterdeck language and expensive jewelry—all of which was stolen at one point. We saw a lot them, going out to restaurants together, often Greek, where the evening would end with smashing the crockery. Next door, the penthouse was occupied by Anthony Havelock-Allan, producer of many distinguished films, including *Brief Encounter,* and married to Valerie Hobson. I had first met him in Rome one Christmas when I flew out to discuss a story about the London Zoo with Ralph Smart, who was in Assisi directing for him the charming Paul Gallico story *Never Take No for an Answer.* I talked over various projects with Tony at Lowndes Square. He and Anthony Asquith were in love with Garrett Mattingly's book *The Defeat of the Spanish Armada,* and I remember a session at which they vied with each other in detailing the complicated relationships of the royalty and other historical characters involved. In a very different direction, I tried to interest Tony in filming the ribald and racy *Mr. Sponge's Sporting Tour*. As a Durham man he was amused by my interest in Soapy Sponge but had reservations about making a picture so largely concerned with fox hunting.

I first met Maite's parents, now reconciled to the loss of their daughter, in the spring of 1957 when on a belated honeymoon we continued into Spain after parting with the Furses at Collioure. Our next visit was to Torre del Mar, then a hamlet on the shore north of Malaga, where we took a villa by the sea for two months so that I could work on a film treatment about El Cid, the legendary Spanish hero. I can still see our charming French au pair (at whose family's chateau—nonetheless—we had stayed on the drive down) wheeling our howling nine-month-old around the geranium-fringed patio while I toiled over Evariste Levi Provençale's monumental *Histoire de l'Espagne musulmane*. It turned out to be lost endeavor, because I was pipped to the post by Samuel Bronsten's epic, with Charlton Heston and Sophia Loren. Years later I met Bronsten in London, where he visited us at Lowndes Square with his entourage to discuss a film about the *Reyes Católicos*, Ferdinand and Isabella, but by then he was no longer the maestro who had built the huge standing sets outside Madrid, and the idea came to nothing.

A second Spanish project was more successful. I had been approached by an American businessman working in Madrid about doing an English adaptation of a book by the famous Spanish cartoonist Mingote of ABC. *La Historia de la Gente* was a satirical world history in cartoons accompanied by suitably ironic text. I liked the idea, and we invited Mingote to stay with us at Torre del Mar to discuss simplifying the book, which was very long, and adding material aimed at foreign readers. We duly picked him up from Malaga, and he was as witty as his drawings and very good company. Maite sat in to help out with my Spanish; Mingote and I saw eye to eye, and the new material was agreed. However, Torre del Mar was a little basic for a sophisticated *madrileño*. The exit pipe from the loo was so narrow that toilet paper could not be flushed away and had to deposited in a large basket (and were subsequently broadcast on the beach by the maid). It fell to Maite to make the somewhat embarrassing explanations. In its new version the book was published in the United Kingdom (in 1960) and United

States as *History for Beginners*—there was even a Japanese edition—and did very well.

During the 1960s, I was involved in various projects with Spanish film directors. We had taken to holidaying in Benicasim, an elegant seaside resort north of Valencia and among the orange groves near Castellón de la Plana. In those days there were no high-rise apartment blocks, and the beach was fringed by dazzlingly white Edwardian or late-Victorian villas, each in its garden shaded by palm trees, many owned by well-to-do Valencians. There was only one hotel, the Voramar (which still survives), with a platform jutting into the sea where there was dancing on Saturday nights, and everyone knew everyone else. We went every year to the same villa, owned by a Galician timber merchant from Valencia, and Maite became the English agent for it and the others that he owned. We soon became part of the community, making friends with the gifted local doctor, exiled for fighting on the wrong side in the Civil War; with Manolo, a plutocratic orange exporter who smoked English pipe tobacco and roared around with his secretary on powerful motorbikes; with Mariano, landowner and ex-cavalryman given to buying religious statuettes by the dozen and presenting his poor wife with children in equal numbers; and with the lawyer in the next villa, one of whose willowy daughters would steal up at Easter and break a hard-boiled egg on one's forehead (my wife tells me that this is an old Spanish tradition, formerly a fertility rite).

Among the summer visitors was a strong film contingent. Rafael Gil, who made musicals with the voluptuous Sara Montiel, had a villa on the front; Luis Berlanga, best known for *Bienvenido Mr. Marshall*, had built himself a house on the rocks overlooking the sea at nearby Oropesa; and we often bumped into Juan Antonio Bardém on the beach or at the Saturday night dances. It was Bardém, director of *Calle Mayor*, starring Betsy Blair from *Marty*, whom we knew best. I had an idea for updating Prosper Merimée's *Colomba*, with its deadly family feud, and transferring the action to the Basque country. Juan Antonio was intrigued, and we went to some lengths to develop a treatment, but, as is apt to happen, we could not interest a distributor. One film on which I worked in Spain and that did come to something was a version of the tragic story of the Spanish princess Inez de Castro, on which I toiled for Vicente Escrivá in Madrid one baking summer while Maite took our small son to the seaside in Santander, where her parents had a house.

Various friends from the entertainment world came to stay with us in Benicasim. Ray Bowers, with whom I had worked on a raft of television series, was as much a Hispanophile as I was myself. He insisted that we climb up to every ruined castle within reach and flirted madly with our French au pair. Leslie Murby from Nelsons, who had published *History for Beginners,* came with his wife and took part with our infant son in racing snails on the terrace. We also explored together the possibilities of the wines made locally by the Padres Carmelitanos at their monastery in the Desierto de las Palmas in the hills above Benicasim. Their speciality was a concentrate shipped to the United Kingdom for home wine makers—of which one of the fathers said with refreshing honesty, "It doesn't make very good wine, but it's delicious spread on bread as jam."

More than once we shared a villa with Lothar Wolff and his wife, Vee. Lothar was assistant producer on *The Roman Spring of Mrs. Stone* and had been with Louis de Rochemont since the days of *March of Time*. He had also worked as an editor for Fritz Lang in Paris and was a gifted filmmaker in his own right and a friend of Lotte Lenya, to whom he introduced us in London. Maite and he had a shared interest in cooking and would make expeditions to the market in Castellón de Plana and take turns at cooking—I remember his magnificent bouillabaisse, made with the splendid local seafood. Our last visit with the Wolffs was in the autumn, when the weather was breaking; the wind would bring down the ripe figs, which burst like bombs on cars parked underneath. There were frequent power failures, when I used to coil pipe cleaners and immerse them in saucers of olive oil in the manner of a Roman lamp.

Another visitor was Clive Nicholas, a power behind the scenes in the film industry. A forceful and outspoken lawyer (who looked after our own small affairs and had arranged Maite's naturalization), he managed the financial affairs of a string of film stars and directors, including Terry Thomas, Glynis Johns, Richard Lester, and Stanley Donen, and was always at hand at times of crisis. Clive flew his own plane and on arrival in London after sessions with clients in Paris and Rome, he would ring us and come to dinner at Lowndes Square or, alternatively, take us out to one of his favorite restaurants, Mr. Chou, or the Chelsea Cloisters, where he had a flat. He had a reputation for being the most ruthless of opponents in a legal dispute, and he was decided in other matters as well. Bidden to dinner by a well-known film producer who liked to hear himself talk, he quietly announced beforehand to the other guests that he himself would say nothing all evening—and did so without his host noticing. On another occasion, when dinner was interminably held up, Clive slipped out, ate at a restaurant, and rejoined the party later. He once flew us out in his executive jet to his house in Provence; there was a doubt about its ability to take off, because it was laden with a heavy lead statue for the garden, but we successfully played hide and seek with the cumulus clouds and landed on open scrub at Manosque. Combative as he seemed to those who did not know him, he was the best of friends.

It was in 1973 that Maite, who had become a formidable cook, joined forces with Catherine O'Brien to write their paperback on Spanish cooking. Catherine and her husband Bill Bachelor were now spending a lot of time in a cottage that they had bought in Mallorca. Both she and Maite had observed with amusement the eating habits of the British on holiday. The visitors to whom Maite let villas in Benicasim, apparently oblivious of the profusion of fish, fresh vegetables and fruit from the Valencian *Huerta* in the open markets, would arrive with their cars loaded with canned baby food and other comestibles from the United Kingdom. In the restaurant they blanched at anything with, or (like paella) possibly containing, tentacles. The recipes in *Spanish Cooking at Home and on Holiday* were authentic but simple, so that they could, if necessary, be prepared on the butane gas cooker of a holiday apartment. Published as a Pan paperback, it caught on at once and was later expanded and reprinted in hardback. To this day we have friends with tattered copies who regard it as their bible. At the same time I was developing an interest in Spanish wines, then an untouched subject, and published the first of many books about them, also in 1973. From now on, most of our visits to Spain were to research further books, sometimes written in collaboration.

The most elaborate of these expeditions was a comprehensive circuit of Spain to gather material for a book on the Paradors. When I had driven with Norman Todd through France and Spain to Lisbon in

1952, the roads had been primitive and potholed; even the main road from San Sebastian to Madrid was unmetaled, on occasion wandering through a farmyard with chickens flying up at the approach of a car, and ending up as a causeway with stone sets on the outskirts of Madrid. There were no service stations in 1952, only a rusting unattended petrol pump every fifty kilometers or so. The accommodation in the interior of the country had not improved greatly since Richard Ford wrote his *Handbook for Travellers in Spain* in 1845, and the bedrooms in a typical *fonda* contained little except the bed and a stand for hanging one's clothes. To remedy this situation the Ministerio de Información y Turismo had inaugurated along major tourist routes luxurious hotels known as Paradors, installed in meticulously restored castles, monasteries, and palaces. In 1952 there had been only twenty-six of them; Norman and I stayed in one of the first, installed in the great Castle of Ciudad Rodrigo on the Portuguese frontier. The Paradors and the simpler Albergues proved enormously popular with foreign visitors; by 1976 there were ninety-six, and Maite and I thought that it would be fascinating to write a book about them and their historical associations.

So it was that we found ourselves in a flat near the bullring in Madrid and with Julian Ashby, a director of Macmillans. With an introduction from the Spanish ambassador in London, Don Manuel Fraga, took him to the *ministerio*, where we were ushered into the presence of the minister of tourism in person. He approved the project, offered all the facilities we needed, and made Julian's day by promising to order large numbers of books. He was as good as his word; the ministry laid on an official car and chauffeur, and for four or five weeks we drove the length and breadth of Spain, covering some ten thousand kilometers, as I remember, and staying at all of the thirty or so establishments described in the book. I ferreted out the history of the buildings, took photographs, and investigated the local wines, while Maite looked into the cuisine and local dishes.

The wine trips, too, took us to every corner of Spain, from Galicia in the north to Jerez de la Frontera and its sherry bodegas in the south. These trips were not without their hazards. Bidden to the 150th-anniversary celebrations of the sherry firm Gonzalez Byass in Madrid, I was slated to conduct a tasting of their Riojas. I had caught a cold after tramping round vineyards in Portugal in the rain, and just before I was due to step up on to the platform I developed a bad nosebleed. I could smell nothing, but fortunately I knew the wines and bluffed my way through. As I did not like any of them, the nosebleed was the perfect excuse!

One person we always made a point of seeing in Madrid—when she was not away on some provincial tour of Shakespeare or Lope de Vega—was my dear actress friend from Venezuela, Natalia. After she divorced her French husband, who had become art editor of *Réalités*, and was rediscovered by Catherine O'Brien on the location of *Richard III*, she married a Spanish theatrical impresario and settled in Madrid. It was a somewhat uneasy partnership. Between them they owned a small cinema in the Plaza de Santa Ana, which they converted into a theater. Natalia was still devoted to the classics, old or modern, and at times I would get in touch with Peggy Ramsay, the London literary agent, on her behalf to ask for permission to perform a Pinter play. Unfortunately, one could not keep a theater open in Madrid with Pinter or Ibsen, and her husband Andrés Magdaleno would regularly put on a striptease or bedroom farce to pay the bills. The only play that I ever saw there was *El Sereno*. A *sereno* was a night porter holding the keys of a group of flats—so the possibilities for Andrés were obvious. Whenever we turned up in Madrid, they would drop everything and invite us to dinner at Valentín, a restaurant near the theater, once patronized by Hemingway and the hangout of theater people and bullfighters and their *aficionados*. Then we heard rumors that they were deep in debt, and next that they had left for Venezuela. Since then, nothing—and I fear that this time even Catherine O'Brien will be unable to help. I miss Natalia, who appeared and shone, then disappeared into the dark, like a shooting star. Let us hope that she finally achieved her ambition of creating a Venezuelan National Theater.

CHAPTER TEN

~

Monsters and Little Green Men

Hollywood has often been called a dream factory, a description more apt when the studios were turning out fairy tales like *It Happened One Night* or *Gentlemen Prefer Blondes* than today, when the dreams so often emerge as nightmares. Nevertheless, the tradition continues in the most literal sense at Disney, and even with the occasional lapses into never-never land, such as *Pretty Woman*, *Crocodile Dundee*, or *While You Were Sleeping*.

A fairy tale is not, of course, the same thing as a legend or a myth, though the story of *Jason and the Argonauts*, which I was asked to develop as a film, has elements of all three. It is, in fact, very difficult to define a myth or to explain how they originated. They are of different sorts and often involve personification of the forces of nature in the form of gods, in the guise of larger-than-life human beings. The most illuminating explanation I have come across is that of Professor H. J. Rose, a colleague of my father at St. Andrews University, to whose book *A Handbook of Greek Mythology* I turned when given the commission. He pointed out that natural phenomena give rise both to science and myths, and that a myth is the result of "imagination working on the facts of experience"—for example, in attributing rain to the sky god, Zeus, pouring down water through a perforated tub.

Considerations of this sort may be stimulating to a scriptwriter, but they are not to a movie producer, whose overriding objective is a box office hit. Mine, in this case, was Charles Schneer, a seasoned Hollywood operator who made pictures for release by Columbia and who, for reasons I never knew, had settled in London. His longtime partner—with whom he made a string of pictures, including the *Seventh Voyage of Sinbad, First Men in the Moon* (in which I also had a hand), and *Clash of the Titans*—was the ingenious Ray Harryhausen, also from the United States, who had invented a process christened "Dynamation" and later "Superdynamation." These combined live action and actors with models of dragons, birds, giants, etc., which he made from a rubberlike material and could manipulate by hand, shooting frame by frame in the manner of a cartoon film.

Charles was of the Hollywood persuasion that a script cannot be rewritten too often, and the writers on the credits of his films rarely met. I, in fact, was introduced to him early in 1962 by the gifted Ray Bowers, with whom, as script editor, I had worked on *Robin Hood* and other television series. Ray had written a first script of *Jason* but bowed out because he lost patience with what he saw as the literal-minded approach to the film—and more particularly, he had little time for his namesake, the endearing Ray Harryhausen, whose real flair, as he saw it, lay in inventing a process that procured him a paycheck only months after main shooting had finished, while he inched on his figurines a single frame at a time.

What I was required to deliver was a fast-moving adventure story with plenty of scope for spectacular special effects. Without straying from the legend there was, of course, plenty of scope for these, with sequences such as the descent of the Harpies on the blind Phineus, the passage of the Argo through the Clashing Rocks, the battle with the armed warriors who sprang from the dragon's seed, and the encounter with the bronze giant, Talos—though this we placed on the outward voyage. Once the fleece was gained, the warriors had been worsted, and boy had got girl in the shape of Medea, it was clearly time for the end titles!

Variety described the picture as "a choice hot weather attraction for the family trade—a sure delight for the kiddies and a diverting spectacle for adults with a taste for fantasy and adventure." High commendation from Hollywood, but as a writer I had tried for a little more. I had long been enamored of Greek mythology, of Ezra Pound's "bright gods and Grecian"; of *The Golden Bough* and Sir James Frazer's "gorgeous drapery of mythic fancy . . . a train of gods and goddesses . . . fashioned out of the shifting panorama of the seasons"; and of the "maiden and mistress of the months and stars" of Swinburne's *Atalanta in Calydon*.

So as to give the narrative more depth and to suggest the relation of the mortals to the gods, I retained a series of scenes from Ray Bowers's earlier script, cutting from the adventures of the Argonauts to scenes on Mount Olympus, with the gods and goddesses actively rooting for their favorites, counseling them, as did Hera from the speaking prow of the Argo, or actually intervening, as when Poseidon emerged from the waters to hold back the Clashing Rocks.

We were justified, I think, in this, because Greek mythology is full of encounters between gods and mortals, not least in the amorous adventures of Zeus himself, who listed among his conquests Niobe, Europe, Alcmene, Antiope, and Danae. His seduction, in the shape of a swan, of Leda resulted in the birth of Helen, whose elopement with Paris led to the Trojan War and the wholesale involvement, on one side or the other, of the whole hierarchy of Olympus. On occasion we arranged for Jason himself to be summoned to Olympus and to engage in dialogue with the gods. This, at least, met with the entire approval of Ray Harryhausen, because it enabled him very simply to portray, by using oversize props, Jason as a pygmy threading his way on the Olympian dining table between goblets as high as himself. I tried to persuade Ray Bowers to take a credit, but he refused, and when I reported this, an offended Charles Schneer exclaimed, "If that's how he feels!" and promptly picked up a ballpoint and scored out Ray's name on the front of the script.

When all is said and done, it is Ray Harryhausen who must take the major share of the credit for the popularity of pictures like *Sinbad*, *Jason*, and *First Men in the Moon*, with its little green Selenites. He was a Californian and a bachelor when we first met, a lanky James Stewart of a man, with an almost childlike attachment to his monsters and an admiration for the drawings of Gustave Doré, which much influenced his set designs. I remember taking my wife (who hates snakes) to dinner at his flat, when he came up behind her with the green rubber hydra, the guardian of the golden fleece, and frightened the wits out of her. He married shortly afterward, and I have always wondered whether his small daughter was given the monsters to play with, in the manner of the Addams family!

The Rank Organisation, which released the picture in the United Kingdom, had its doubts about *Jason* in the first place and tried it out in Bristol. It proved to be a "sleeper" and has survived to this day, where many more pretentious and expensive productions have been forgotten. Like those Greek deities whose annual ritual reflects the decay and revival of vegetation, it regularly reappears in movie houses and on television at holiday times to divert children of all ages.

Doffing my cap in the direction of Ray Harryhausen; the producer, Charles Schneer; the director, Don Chaffey; and Todd Armstrong, Nancy Kovak, Honor Blackman, and the others who played in it—I think that *Jason* was saved from turning into just another spectacular action picture by the irony of the scenes on Olympus and the treatment of the gods. Their dialogue, at least, was fairly sophisticated. My favorite line (written by Ray Bowers and not myself) was Hera's rejoinder to a masterful Zeus that the gods will survive only as long as mortals believe in them—which embodies a truth about religious belief beyond that of the Greeks.

Hard on the success of *Jason*, Schneer asked me if I would take on another subject, *First Men in the Moon*, based on the novel by H. G. Wells. Again there was an existing script, this time by the accomplished science fiction writer, Nigel Kneale. It was stylish and amusing, but evidently it did not allow sufficient scope for Harryhausen's special effects, which, of course, from the point of view of the producers, was the raison d'être for the picture. By now I was an old hand at Dynamation and was able to save Ray a lot of time by specifying in the script live action, back projection, matte shots, oversize props, actual dynamation with models, and the rest.

With unexpected topicality, the picture began with shots of the arrival of the rocket ship on the moon, which looked uncannily similar to those of the American landing on the moon just days before the film's release. However, in the words of the *Times*, "This show of documentary realism is soon abandoned; the first explorers discover to their horror that they are not the first, for there awaiting them is a small Union Jack and a note claiming the moon for Queen Victoria. A chase back to earth (Dymchurch specifically) reveals the last survivor of an earlier group ready to tell all, and off we go on a course of early Wells, neatly renovated by Mr. Nigel Kneale and Mr. Jan Read."

The special effects required by the underground city of the Selenites and its insectlike inhabitants gave Ray Harryhausen a lot of fun, but I suspect that, like myself, Nigel Kneale, whom to my regret I never met, was more interested in the eccentric inventor Cavor, splendidly played by Lionel Jeffries. As the *Hollywood Reporter* opined, "The pseudo scientific apparatus of the nineteenth century is much more intriguing than today's push-button computer models. Some of the scenes of Jeffries building his equipment are comic delights, particularly a blast furnace in the center of a chintz-decked library, and the spaceship's home in the greenhouse."

The picture ends with a sequence in which the present-day astronauts descend into the lunar city, only to find a half-choked shaft and the desiccated remains of the Selenites, evidently wiped out by a catastrophic epidemic. This gives rise to a last and telling line (Nigel Kneale's) when Edward Judd, the only survivor of the original expedition, is interrogated and remarks, "Cavor *did* have the most terrible cold."

Schneer asked me to work on a number of other projects, including the Jules Verne story *The Light at the Edge of the World* and *The Saint with Red Hands*, about which I can remember nothing at all, except that we met at Schneer's house in Campden Hill, where his wife, a charming lady of the ruling Columbia dynasty, had assembled an impressive collection of modern paintings. I do, however, have vivid recollections of meetings on *You Must Be Joking*, at which the director, a young and confident Michael Winner, kept pressing for changes to the script, insisting, "Charles, I guarantee this will knock 'em in the aisles." When, finally, a character from north of the border had, as I saw it, been divested of any trace of Scottishness, I wrote to Charles saying that he had been left with nothing but his kilt and asking for permission to bow out.

Looking through my diaries for 1962 to 1964, when I worked on some half-dozen projects for Schneer, I see that I had numerous other irons in the fire. This is of the essence of freelance writing; when times are good, the phone keeps ringing and one can pick and choose. Then there are spells when it does not ring at all, and one bombards one's long-suffering agent with outlines and treatments for films or television series. Two such were *Race in the Dark*, a thriller set against the background of the late-nineteenth-century railway races to Aberdeen, and a television series with a Riviera setting, on which I joined forced with Pennington Richards, who had photographed *White Corridors*. I had an interesting flight to Nice, when I found myself sitting opposite Robert Morley and Jack Hylton, who had produced the stage version of the *Blue Lamp*; Penny and I stayed on board his motor yacht at Villefranche, making expeditions to Cannes, Nice, and Monte Carlo in search of local color. It was a charming holiday, and I duly produced some dozen Maugham-like stories, but they failed to find a buyer.

At that point I was approached by the BBC about a new version of *Sherlock Holmes*. Played by Douglas Wilmer as Holmes and Nigel Stock as Dr. Watson, this was a most enjoyable series to write—and of course much easier than inventing original stories. It was edited by John Gould, whom I liked and respected. At the time he was new at the game—like myself at Gainsborough years before—and it was not so long before that he had found a summer job in the food department in Harrods. He was serving there one day when a lady turned up, and, without looking up, he asked what he could do for her—to which she replied, "It's your mother, John. May I take you out to lunch?" John became a talented writer and was soon elected chairman of the Screenwriters' Guild. He died tragically young of cancer.

The person, apart from my agent, Margery Vosper, with whom I was most continuously involved at this period was Theodora Olembert. Theodora first came into my life in 1956, shortly before I married. It was a thin patch for scriptwriting, and when the phone rang one day at Shrewsbury House and a thick, foreign voice tumbled out of it asking if I would be free to write a documentary film about Bernard Shaw, I thought, "Why not?" After all, documentary had been my first love. Little did I know of the trials and tribulations in which this would involve me.

Theodora, born in Poland, had married a French diplomat and worked in the films division of UNESCO before settling in London and setting up Triangle Films to make a series of high-minded documentaries, including *Bernard Shaw, Chopin, The Chinese Theatre, Edith Piaf, Salvador Dalí*, and *Is Venice Sinking?*—in all of which willy-nilly I found myself involved. An earlier picture, *Leonardo da Vinci*, had won a gold medal at the Venice Film Festival. I was in due course even persuaded to become codirector of her company. Theodora was a courageous and determined woman who had set herself the nearly impossible task of raising money to make "art films" and persuading commercially minded distributors to show them.

In her late forties, when I first met her, she was short and stout and took little care about dress or hair, single-mindedly devoting all her energies to film, particularly documentary. That was about all we shared. Whereas I was always punctilious about turning up on time, Theodora was congenitally unable to appear for an interview, however important, less than half an hour late. I remember occasions when I waited as long as I could, then went in alone and on occasion, as with David Deutsch at Anglo-Amalgamated, had to leave without her putting in an appearance. When we invited her to dinner, we simply began without her; as she was not much interested in food, Maite would cook her a French omelette when she eventually arrived. She had unlimited access to free tickets at the cinema and, being a kind person, would invite our small son to see, say, *How the West Was Won*—and then drive him to distraction by failing to appear until well after the picture had begun, by which time he was clamoring to go home. Having made me her codirector, she expected me to write the commentaries for her films and also letters of any importance, keeping me on the phone for literally an hour at a time, especially at mealtimes. Triangle was in no position to pay for any of these services, and you may well ask why I continued with her. I suppose the answer is that in spite of everything I liked her and admired her quixotic rejection of everything commercial.

She had a wide circle of friends in literary and film circles, and (often over what seemed to be her one weakness, pastries and sweet liqueurs at her flat in Primrose Hill) I met Vercors, the French Resistance writer, and his wife Rita Barisse, translator of Marcel Pagnol's *The Days Were Too Short*; Jacques Demy, the gifted director of *Les Parapluies de Cherbourg*; Dilys Powell and Caroline Lejeune, the film critics; Peter Cooke; Andrew Sinclair, then just down from Cambridge and beginning as a writer;

Ann Todd; and many others. Robert Hamer, the brilliant Ealing director of *Kind Hearts and Coronets*, was a particular concern of hers because of his drinking problem. Apart from myself, she relied for practical support on the merchant banker George Szpiro, who was married to her cousin, and on John Terry of the National Film Finance Corporation. The hardheaded John, also a good friend of Robert Hamer, whose job it was to assess films and advance money for what he regarded as worthwhile and viable ones, I think felt about her much as I did. Certainly he helped her regularly with her films, although the amounts may have been only a few thousand pounds, and talked to her like a Dutch uncle.

My first assignment for her was typical. There was already a rough cut of *Bernard Shaw*, of which the highlights were filmed interviews with Shaw himself. However, it lacked shape and drive, and before I could get to work it was a question of sitting at a moviola with a cutter in Dean Street and reconstructing the film as best we could with the existing material. This done, we timed the various sequences, and I wrote commentary to fit. Commentary and music were recorded at the same time, the commentator watching the film from a glass box. Music tended to be expensive and live performers out of the question; for *Bernard Shaw* I myself provided 78 rpm records of Mozart's *Clarinet Concerto*. They reproduced perfectly—though I am afraid that Triangle did not seek to reimburse the record company!

The high-water mark of my involvement with Triangle took place in the autumn of 1958, when Theodora announced that she intended to make a film about the Venice Film Festival and asked me, as of yesterday, to accompany her. We were on holiday in Scotland at the time, and it was a question of leaving my wife and one-month-old baby with my parents. However, wracking my brains as to how Triangle could for once make something that cinemas might book, I bethought myself of a story I had written for the unmade Riviera series. It was about an English director who goes to the Cannes festival to find a starlet for his new film, without success until he drops in at an English tearoom and spots a girl who has taken a job as a waitress, hoping to attract notice at the festival. It could easily be adapted to Venice, was simple enough for a small budget, and allowed plenty of scope for festival background.

With some reservations, because she fought shy of anything with a prospect of returns at the box office, Theodora fell in with the idea and engaged a French documentary director, of whom she had good reports but had not actually met. He in turn undertook to engage a French starlet for the ingénue, and Jon van Eyssen (later head of Columbia in the United Kingdom), who was already in Venice, volunteered to play the English director of my story. I had my misgivings about the French director and arranged for Gerry Bryant, my Gainsborough friend (who by now had directed the successful *Tommy Steele Story*), to come for the trip and help out with the production and the script, not as yet written. It was just as well, because the French documentarist proved incapable of directing a foot of film, and the starlet turned out to be his girlfriend—she was as ugly as sin and spoke English with a thick nasal accent. There was nothing much we could do about her at this late stage, but we duly settled in at a hotel on the Lido, and Gerry picked up a lot of useful location footage.

The production had its moments of comedy and drama. We co-opted extras and bit parts on the spot—as, for example, in the last sequence, when Jon van Eyssen, having made up his mind about the girl, returns to the teashop, only to find that she has run out of funds and has just left for the station. He makes a dash for a water taxi to take him across the lagoon but is beaten to it by an Italian businessman. For this last character we simply accosted a well-dressed man in black with a despatch case and asked if he would cooperate. He displayed signs of nervousness but agreed. However, when Gerry wanted to repeat the shot, he burst out that he was on his way to a funeral and departed at speed.

Then there was the occasion in St. Mark's Square, where we had set up to shoot a brief scene outside Thomas Cook. Theodora meanwhile spotted an Italian friend going into the Hotel Cipriani and vanished. We waited for ten minutes, then I told the cameraman to go ahead. As we were finishing, she reappeared and flew into a fury, saying that we had no business to shoot without her and finally telling me that I was no longer codirector of her company. By now, what with presenting her with a script, arranging for Gerry's services gratis, and coping with the useless French director and his ugly girlfriend, I had had my fill. Saying to her that I would take the next plane home, I was on my way to the BEA office on the other side of the square when she caught up with me and apologized.

It remained to shoot a couple of dialogue scenes in the tearoom, and for this we booked a small studio in London and flew over our starlet. She spent the night on the town and turned up late, with the father and mother of a hangover. I did my best to save the film by getting hold of the expert Jocelyn Jackson, sister of Pat, who had directed *White Corridors*, to cut it, but between the girl's appearance and thick accent, it was now beyond any of our efforts. Theodora eventually utilized the footage to make a documentary entitled *Is Venice Sinking?*—for which I duly wrote the commentary.

Some years later and again on holiday in St. Andrews, I received another phone call urging me to join her in Cadaqués in Spain, where she was about to shoot a film about Salvador Dalí. With a *Finlay* script to write and with memories of Venice, this time I begged off. From what I heard later, it was an eventful production, with Dalí opening his studio to them and playing up to his full bent. Highlights of the footage were the shots where he created a picture by hurling live fish at the canvas and squashing them, and where he was hoisted into the air by a helicopter with cords attached to his burgeoning moustache. I was drawn into endless discussions about the film; it was never completed, but Theodora recouped some of the cost by selling the famous helicopter shot and other footage.

The time came at last when I felt that I must resign as her codirector. I had no wish to abandon her, time consuming as the association was, but in signing the company's accounts each year (at the eleventh hour) it increasingly came home to me that I might find myself with financial liabilities into the bargain. With a young wife and child, this was something I could not risk. She was, of course, outraged and bitterly hurt at my decision, especially because, as she then told me, she had left the rights in various of her films to our son, John Carlos—largely because of whom I had bowed out. A year of two later, I did in fact, write her a treatment for a film about Shelley and used my best efforts to get John Terry and George Szpiro to back it. I was sorry that it was never made, as it had distinct possibilities.

Theodora Olembert played a large part in our lives over a dozen years or so, and irritated as one often was with the demands she made on one's time and the impracticality of so many of her projects, Maite and I both ended up with great affection for her, with her self-imposed crusade. I have never met anyone else remotely like her.

CHAPTER ELEVEN

Where We Came In

When television arrived in the late forties and early fifties with BBC broadcasts from Alexandra Palace, few of us in showbiz took it very seriously. The clumsy sets, with their small screens and pygmy performers, seemed toylike. When I eventually plumped for one it was for something in advance of its time, a Decca projection set, which showed the pictures on a five-by-four-foot cinema screen. It was novelty enough for Rex Harrison and Kay Kendall to walk down the Embankment with me from Roger Furse's studio to my cottage in Dilke Street to watch it in action.

As regards writing for television, movies always remained my first love, although like most scriptwriters I was soon involved, since with the vicissitudes of the British film industry it became increasingly difficult to make a living from writing film scripts alone (and is now, of course, impossible, except in Hollywood).

My first attempt at writing for television, and the first-ever police series, was one of six half-hour parts called *Pilgrim Street*, screened in 1952. I was recommended to the BBC by my friend Percy Fearnley, the public-relations man at Scotland Yard with whom I had worked on *The Blue Lamp*. I based it on the station at Gerald Road in Pimlico—and did my research thoroughly, to the extent of being thrown smartly to the ground by a woman police constable in a demonstration of unarmed defense and suffering minor injuries! At the same time, I went out to Alexandra Palace to see television being made and sat in on a musical program featuring Vera Lynn, the wartime forces' favorite. I remember thinking at the time that it was all very much like shooting a film, but on a smaller scale; scripting too amounted to much the same thing, except that one was limited to small sets and fewer characters. *Pilgrim Street* was recorded at Shepherd's Bush studios, by this time sold by Rank to the BBC, on one of the stages I knew so well from my days at Gainsborough. It was very well directed by a young Irishman, Kevin Sheldon, whom I liked.

Following on from *Pilgrim Street*, I was a couple of years later asked to write another police series *Fabian of the Yard*. It was on a real case of Fabian's that I had based *The Blue Lamp*. I now met the bluff and down-to-earth detective superintendent for the first time, downing gin and tonics in the bar at Alexandra Palace. In fact, the stories, like *The Ribbon Track*, were complete fiction and more resembled Sherlock Holmes than actual police work.

I chiefly remember the series for its gentlemanly American producer, John Larkin, a kindred spirit from 20th Century–Fox. He was fascinated with the London restaurant scene, and once a week we would eat at the Elysée, or the Jardin des Gourmets, L'Escargot, Wheelers, the Braganza, the Ivy, Pruniers, the Gay Hussar, or one of the rest. Being tall like myself, with long legs, he always used to reserve a table for three or four and was adept at fending off waiters with his dismissive Yankee drawl, as once at a crowded Rules off the Strand, when pressed about the missing guests. On one occasion at Hatchetts I had ordered a bottle of Mouton Cadet. I saw at once that it had a scaly deposit, but the wine was fresh and good. When the wine waiter belatedly noticed the deposit and, ignoring our protests, officiously whipped the bottle away, John saw red. He bided his time and ordered Calvados as a liqueur. It was perfect, but he beckoned to the waiter and said poker-faced: "What is this? Applejack?" The wine waiter, the maîtred', and the manager all in turn arrived at the table and tasted it—from John's glass—but he held firm, demanding and obtaining restitution.

Once I had broken the ice, other television assignments came thick and fast. One of these was *Robin Hood,* made in 1956–57, the longest-running and most popular of all the early filmed television series. It was produced for Lew Grade's ITC by Hannah Weinstein, a dynamic American woman, who, like other writers and directors with liberal views, transferred to the United Kingdom to escape hounding by the House Committee on Un-American Activities.

Her script editor was the forthright and talented Australian Ray Bowers, soon to become a close friend. Like many of his compatriots he lived in Earls Court, and he was married to a statuesque blonde who had been tennis champion of South Australia. He was unlucky in love: there was a protracted divorce, and no sooner was it finished than the pretty German girl who had seen him through it and whom he hoped to marry abruptly left him to his "barge hound" and a gloomy ground-floor mansion flat. Perhaps his habit of working through the night and his taste for Scotch had something to do with it, because he was a vibrant and stimulating person. It was he who later walked out of *Jason and the Argonauts* and launched me on my encounter with Superdynamation. Some of Ray's best work was for the stylish series about the machinations of the business world, *The Power Game*.

It was on a second series, *The Four Just Men*, that I got to know Hannah rather better and more particularly her brother, Seymour Dorner, who managed her business affairs. A former executive of Gimbels, the New York department store, he was a charming man married to an equally charming wife. They had three children of about the same age as our own son, and they often played together in the park—all through my time in films and television, I found that what began as professional relationships often developed into real friendships. We still see Ruth Dorner on trips to New York.

The Four Just Men was based on a novel by Edgar Wallace and starred Jack Hawkins, Richard Conte, Ben Gazzara, and, unexpectedly, Dan Dailey, of the long legs and boaters. As happens in series of this kind, the Wallace stories soon ran out, and the new material had to be tailored to the contrasting personalities of the stars, who took turns in playing the lead in different episodes. In charge of scripts was another refugee from Paramount and the House Committee on Un-American Activities, Ian Hunter, who had written Audrey Hepburn's enchanting *Roman Holiday*. He was quiet and reserved, with an underlying and unsuspected sense of humor. I still remember the family Thanksgiving dinner to which we were invited—the turkey, stuffed with cranberries at one end and oysters at the other, and the astonishment of my Spanish wife at being served tiny liqueur glasses of red wine to wash down the repast. My friend Pat Jackson, for whom Ian wrote a film, found him unduly staid and serious and quotes him as saying, "I don't travel well." I rather feel that he missed the irony.

Between films I worked on an assortment of TV series over the next years, including *Skyport* for Granada, again edited by Ray Bowers; *Zero One* for M-G-M; the BBC's *Flying Swan,* starring Margaret Lockwood and her daughter as proprietors of a country hotel; *Detective Story,* about which I can remember nothing at all; and *Danger Man.*

The last was produced for Lew Grade by Ralph Smart, the Australian director from Gainsborough. After a stint in 1954 when we were both without assignments, we collaborated on three film scripts (one of which, *The Flying Scot,* was later sold and made by Anglo-Amalgamated). Since those hard times, when I was myself reduced to selling a treasured gouache of Ascot Races by Raoul Dufy to make ends meet, Ralph had found his métier in filmed television. Beginning with *William Tell,* he went on to produce the entertaining and highly successful *Danger Man* with Patrick MacGoohan, which was shown all over the world.

Ralph and his wife Meg had a passion for buying houses, doing them up and then moving on. During the time I knew them they successively bought and occupied a flat in Fulham Road and houses in the Isle of Wight, Nettlebed in Oxfordshire, the Costa Brava, and the French Pyrenees—not to mention establishments in his native Australia, to which they returned at intervals. Nettlebed was the one I knew best and, like everything they took in hand, was immaculate. It was a spacious, low-built house set in rolling, wooded countryside; they had installed under-floor heating and a beautiful slate fireplace in the long, airy sitting room with an unbroken expanse of glass down one side. The kitchen had been remodeled to take an Aga stove, in which I cooked the egg and bacon for breakfast when I stayed with them. Meg, when she was not cutting stencils for duplicating our scripts, seemed constantly to be stripping window frames with a blowgun or painting bedrooms.

By the late 1960s, filmed television had come into its own. Productions became increasingly more elaborate, and instead of the half-hour of the early series, episodes now ran to fifty minutes—to allow for commercial breaks. Lew Grade's ITC had more or less cornered the British market and had broken into the United States with its "mid-Atlantic" series, permanently maintaining soundstages, offices, and cutting rooms at Pinewood Studios to make them. With one of these, *Man in a Suitcase*, produced by Sidney Cole, a former producer at Ealing Studios, I became closely involved. It was an amiable enough hit-and-bash thriller series, still regularly rerun, and I first contributed to it as a freelance, working with its American editor (now, in view of the enhanced status of such series, known as a "story consultant"). Stanley Greenberg was one of the brightest and most fertile writers I ever knew, but after twenty-six of the thirty-nine episodes he decided that he had had enough and wanted to go back to America and movies.

In doing so, he wished his job on me. It was in fact no sinecure, since as the operation was geared, each episode was scheduled for ten working days in the studio, after which, come hell or high water, another script had to be ready for shooting. Story consultant or not, there were occasions when one had to do more than see writers and commission scripts, but roll up one's sleeves and write. On one such, on a Friday evening when shooting was due to start the following Monday, Sidney Cole, in consultation with myself and the director, Peter Duffell, decided that the script would really not wash and must be rewritten in its entirety. Fortunately Peter, apart from being a director, was an experienced scriptwriter, and it was agreed that I should take Acts I and III and he Acts II and IV, rewrite them over the weekend, and meld them first thing on the Monday morning. It was a feverish weekend for us both, but we duly delivered, and when the film was in the can the powers-that-be at ITC judged it one of the best episodes of the series. (I never met the legendary cigar-smoking Lew Grade in person, but after visiting the Canaries in aid of a piece for *Harpers & Queen* about a Cuban expatriate making the only authentic Upmann cigars, I sent Lord Grade, as he now was, three cigars even larger than anything I had seen him smoke. He was duly appreciative!)

Man in a Suitcase was based on the very simple, and hardly original, premise of an American freebooter, played by Richard Bradford, taking on dangerous assignments wherever they cropped up (my wife acted as technical and dialogue adviser on an episode shot by Charles Crichton, a survivor from Ealing, with the leafy surroundings of Pinewood doing duty for Spain). Nevertheless, the idea worked, the stories were intriguing, and the series caught on. I could never really fathom the formula of its successor, the *Strange Report*, a subsequent ITC series that I was asked to edit together with Ed de Blasio from Hollywood, who had worked on *Mission Impossible* and was later to produce the Joan Collins epic *Dynasty*. The lead was played by the respected English actor Anthony Quayle, but the stories hinged on a "do good" element, which was to my mind the kiss of death. In the event the series was a complete flop, but long before that I had walked out. On the afternoon that I resigned and vacated my office at Pinewood, I was nearly killed on the way home when the windshield of my car exploded and I swerved off the motorway at speed.

The near accident was a turning point, and though I was to work on a few more TV projects, *Strange Report* brought to a head a growing disillusionment with television in general. Fortunately, I had an alternative open to me in the shape of books on wine, travel, and history, and articles in *History Today*. There was, however, a final chapter to the story of my first love, movies.

Louis de Rochemont, who had given me my first opportunity at 20th Century–Fox, was by now an old man, but twenty-five years on he had lost none of his zest for filmmaking. During those years we had never lost touch; I reworked the script for him when he came to London to make *The Roman Spring of Mrs. Stone*, and he was later engaged with John Halas and Joy Bachelor on a feature-length cartoon of George Orwell's *Animal Farm*. On these visits he usually put himself into the Hyde Park Hotel, the Capital, or the Carlton Tower, round the corner from our flat in Lowndes Square, so as to be close to us. When he came to town, one had always to be prepared to drop everything else. With someone as emotional as Louis there were, of course, ups and downs. The worst episode, which blew up like hurricane out of a clear sky, was over his grandson, Shaler. His mother, Louis's daughter Gingie (so nicknamed to distinguish her from her mother Ginnie, or Virginia), whom I very much liked, had married, was long divorced, and was working as a teacher in Rhode Island when the teenage Shaler rang up to say that he was in London with his father; could he come to see us? Naturally, I said yes, but I had a premonition of perils ahead when he asked if he could bring his father too. Drinks at the flat passed off very amicably—the father seemed friendly and civilized enough—but the next thing that happened was an hour-long telephone call from the United States in which Louis denounced him as the deadly enemy of the de Rochemont family and accusing me of trying to drive a wedge between Shaler and Gingie and of stabbing the family in the back. It was all like a family feud from *The Forsyte Saga*.

Caring for Louis, Ginnie, and Gingie as I did, and preposterous as it all was, I was deeply upset. In fact, Louis never referred to the fracas again, and when we next met it was at the Savoy Grill to discuss a project close to his heart. He had for long wanted to make a picture in the style of his early semidocumentary successes *The House on 92nd Street* and *13 Rue Madeleine*. On periodic visits to London and Paris he kept returning to his interest in the German resistance movement and the internal opposition to Hitler during World War II, and now he asked me if I would be interested in preparing a storyline. He left me with a stack of books on the subject and a month or two later phoned to ask if I could fly out to work with him on the project at Blueberry Bank, his house at Newington near Portsmouth, New Hampshire, for which I had such nostalgic memories of Christmas in New England.

Newington was then, in the spring of 1970, still an unspoiled village, and Blueberry Bank at the end of its long tree-lined drive was just as I had remembered it, a low, white, colonial-style mansion. The main change was that Louis had sold off part of the property to an electrical company, which had built a manufacturing plant on the land, but the grounds were extensive, and one did not see it from the house. The children were now grown up and had left home, so Louis, Ginnie, and I were on our own. I soon settled into a pleasant and relaxed routine, discussing the story with Louis and then retiring to my room, with its view over the garden and trees, and going to work with the typewriter. Louis had lost none of his skill in the kitchen, and Ginnie still treated me in her somewhat authoritarian manner as one of her own.

Louis had in the meantime been in touch with Christina Bielenberg over the biography of her husband, Peter, one of the leaders of the resistance, who had been exposed and brutally executed by the Nazis. Our treatment was loosely based on the book, which was well written and human. The work went well, and in ten days or so I had completed a first draft. Louis, who as always relied heavily on Ginnie's judgment, wanted a few days to confer with her. As it happened, my American sister-in-law had a holiday house on Martha's Vineyard down the coast and was holidaying there, so it was arranged that I should take a Greyhound bus and visit her.

I returned to find that they both liked what I had done, and Louis now wanted to look into arrangements for setting up the film before going farther. On the day that we were to drive to Boston and I was to fly home, he cut his hand badly in the kitchen. The doctor bandaged him, but this accident was to have very serious repercussions. Ginnie drove us to Boston for a farewell lunch at Louis's favorite restaurant in the Ritz-Carlton Hotel, after which I took the night plane. It was the last time I was to see him. He suffered complications from his injury and never fully recovered his health; he was therefore unable to proceed with the film. His death was a very great sorrow to me.

Many, many years later, in November 1995, my wife and I were on a visit to our relatives in Boston, and my brother-in-law drove us up to New Hampshire and Vermont to see the last of the fall colors. On our way north we stopped for lunch at Portsmouth, and I thought that I should like to take a look at Blueberry Bank. We duly drove past the huge and now abandoned navy yard and took the road to Newington. It no longer ran through fields as I had last seen it but was continuously bordered by shops, billboards, garages, and secondhand car lots. I was beginning to think we were on the wrong road when down to the right I saw a vast factory. Could this be the electrical works that had been starting up when I visited Louis in 1970? I got Jeff to turn into the concreted entrance. Sure enough, it was an electrical factory, and by rights Blueberry Bank should be a little farther on and on the same side.

I located it by the long drive and the line of trees on either side. We drove to the bottom and rang at the front door that I knew so well. It was answered by a caretaker. He was a friendly man who explained that the house was now a hospitality center for guests of the electrical concern, and when I said that I was a friend of the de Rochemonts and had stayed there in the past, he asked if we would like to look round. It was very much as I remembered it, with the large drawing room, the paneled study where I had made old-fashioneds in the early hours, and the kitchen where Louis's turkey had exploded at Christmas. I asked about the de Rochemonts to be told that Shaler, who had visited us in London, still had a cottage on the grounds but was away, and that his grandmother had long been living in a nursing home and did not see callers. We were about to leave when he asked me if I would sign the visitor's book.

It had a space for the visitor's company and position—I signed it 20th Century–Fox. The chilly wind that had pursued us down the streets of Portsmouth had freshened, and the last leaves were fluttering on the trees in the drive as we turned out and headed north for Vermont.

Index

20th Century–Fox, 13, 15, 16, 34–35, 149

A'Deane, Sarn, 99, 111, 120, 121
Amies, Hardy, 116
Andrews, Dana, 17, 18, 22
Annakin, Ken, 78
Anstey, Edgar, 1
Asquith, Anthony, 124

The Bad Lord Byron, 79
Balcon, Sir Michael, 68, 83, 87, 88, 97
Bardém, Juan Antonio, 126
Barry, Iris, 54
BBC, 101–2, 136, 141, 144
The Beach of Falesa, 80, 81–82, 83
Begley, Ed, 17
Benicasim, film colony in, 126
Bennett, Joan, 58, 59, 60–61
Bernard Shaw, 136, 137, 138
Bielenberg, Christina, 147–48

Blood Orange, 116
The Blue Lamp, 70, 74, 75, 86–91
Blueberry Bank, 31–32, 147, 148–49
Bogarde, Dirk, 78
Boomerang!, 17–25
Bowers, Ray, 127, 132, 133, 134, 143, 144
Box, Betty, 69, 74
Box, Muriel, 73–74, 79, 115
Box, Sydney: and *The Blue Lamp*, 86–88; and his Gainsborough films, 75; and *Street Corner*, 115; announces closure of Gainsborough, 91; as executive producer at Gainsborough, 70; character of, 70; on *The Beach of Falesa*, 81; on Dylan Thomas, 83–84
Bradford, Richard, 145
British Medical Association (BMA), 100
Bronsten, Samuel, 125

Brown, Clarence, 38–39
Brown, Lady Vernon, 111–12
Bryant, Gerry, 75, 91, 139
Bundy, Frank, 73

Carreras, Michael, 116
Carter, Maurice, 97
Castle, Joan, 112
Chaffey, Don, 123
Chayevsky, Paddy, 113
Chrichton, Charles, 145
Christopher Columbus, 79
Clark, Petula, 74, 98
Clarke, T. E. B., 88
Claxton, Dr. Ernest, 100
Cobb, Lee J., 17
Cole, Sidney, 145
Colleran, Bill, 25, 30
Collins, Joan, 113
Commonwealth Fund, 7–8
Cooke, Alistair, 46, 63
Corri, Adrienne, 124
Cruikshank, Andrew, 103, 104
Cummings, Jean, 10
Cummings, Michael, 68, 120

Dalí, Salvador, 140
Danger Man, 144
Darnborough, Anthony, 72, 73
Darnell, Linda, 34–37
Davis, John, 69, 81
Day, Robert, 123
de Blasio, Ed, 146
de Lacey, Phil, 43
de Rochemont, Ginnie, 17, 33, 147, 148, 149
de Rochemont, Louis: accident and death of, 148; and Christmas in New Hampshire, 31–32; and the German resistance movement, 147; and *The March of Times* and early feature films, 16; and projected production of *Spoonhandle*, 30; at the Carlton Tower, 56; at the Waldorf Astoria, 25–29; dislike of Hollywood, 33–34; produces *Boomerang!*, 17–25; produces *The Roman Spring of Mrs. Stone*, 55, 146; quarrel with Zanuck and exit from Fox, 41–42
de Rochemont, Shaler, 146, 149
de Zulueta, Father, 111, 112
Deutsch, David, 137
Dixon of Dock Green, 86
documentary films, in the United Kingdom, 1
Donald, James, 98
Dorner, Seymour, 143
Dors, Diana, 75
Dr. Finlay's Casebook, 101–4
Duffell, Peter, 145

Ealing Studios, xiii, 88, 89
Eldridge, Florence, 79
Encore, 78
Escrivá, Vicente, 126
Evans, Sir Charles, 124
export embargo on American films, 68–69, 91
extras, rates of pay, 38
Eyssen, John van, 139

Fabian of the Yard, 142
Fearnley, Percy, 86, 141
Festival of Britain, 92
First Men in the Moon, 134–35
Flaherty, Robert, 54
flood disaster, Dutch, 116
The Flying Scot, 144

Forever Amber, 34
The Four Just Men, 143
Furse, Ines, 111, 112–13
Furse, Roger, 110, 112–14, 125

Gainsborough Pictures (1928) Ltd., 68–69
Garbo, Greta, 14
Gardner, Ava, 92–93
Gaumont-British Picture Corporation, 67, 71
Goldwyn, Sam, 14–15
Gordon, Richard, 123
Gould, John, 136
Gould, Sheila, 121
Grade, Lew, 143, 145
Great Western Railway, 5–6
Green, Harry, 101
Greenberg, Stanley, 145
Greene, Henry, 108
Grierson, John, 1, 54
Grip of the Strangler (The Haunted Strangler), 123

Hamer, Robert, 138
Hammer Films, 116
Hardy, Thomas, 5
Harrison, Rex, 141
Harryhausen, Ray, 132–35
Hartmann, Cyril, 70, 73
Havelock-Allan, Anthony, 124–25
Haworth, Sir Norman, F. R. S., 8
Hepburn, Katharine: and *The Great British Breakfast*, 40; and her arrival in Hollywood, 14; and the "Hollywood Ten," 63; on the set of *Song of Love*, 37–40
"Hollywood Ten," 63
Hoornik, Ed., 116
Hoover, J. Edgar, 16

The House on 92nd Street, 16
Hugget, 88, 91
Hugget family series, 74, 75, 91
Hunter, Ian, 143–44
Hylton, Jack, 89

Inglis, Brian ("one take"), 99
Insurance Company of North America, 43
International House, 45, 49–50
Irvine, Sir James, 7
Is Venice Sinking?, 140
ITC (Incorporated Television Company), 143, 145, 146

J. Arthur Rank Organisation, xiii, 67–69, 94, 95, 96
Jackson, Pat: directs *White Corridors*, 98–99; on Fritz Lang, 66; on Ian Hunter, 144; return from Hollywood, 97
Jago, Jo, 5–6
James, Jocelyn, 109, 114
Janni, Joe, 99
JARO. *See* J. Arthur Rank Organisation
Jason and the Argonauts, 131–34
Jennings, Shirley, 115
Johns, Glynis, 78

Karloff, Boris, 113, 123–24
Kazan, Elia, directs *Boomerang!*, 17–25
Keene, Ralph, 73, 75, 80, 81
Kendall, Kay, 113, 141
Kennedy, Arthur, 17, 25
King's Head and Eight Bells, 98, 105–15
Klinger, Michael, 99
Kneale, Nigel, 134

Korda, Alexander, 8
Krazy Cat, 66

La Historia de la Gente, 125
Lang, Fritz: and conversations in his garden, 62; and his articles on filmmaking, 61; and his classic German films, 58; approach from Gainsborough, 65; critics and misconceptions of, 65–66; directs *Secret beyond the Door*, 50–51; on the British film tax of 1947, 68–69; sets up Diana Film Productions, 58–60
Larkin, John, 109, 142
Laurel Canyon, 57–58
Lawrence, Col. Justin ("Jock"): American representative of Rank Organisation, 13–14; as Hearst reporter, 14; as wartime PR for General Eisenhower, 15; at RKO with Marx brothers and Katharine Hepburn, 14; at Universal, 58; in London, 70; inventor of Goldwynisms, 14–15
Lester, Hugh, 18, 45
Levene, Sam, 17
London Films, xiii
London Hippodrome, 90
Lowndes Square, 122–23

Macgowan, Kenneth, 64, 66
MacKinnon, Alan, 74–75, 91
Malden, Karl, 17
Man in a Suitcase, 145–46
Manjón, Maite (Mrs. Jan Read), 113, 120, 121–23, 125, 127, 128, 145
March, Frederic, 79

Marx, Groucho, 41
Matthews, Jessie, 71
Maugham, Somerset, 72–73
McCarthy, Senator, 62–63
Me and My Bike, 80, 83, 84
Metro-Goldwyn-Mayer (M-G-M), 37–38
Miller, Nat, 123
Mills, Hugh, 78, 106
Mingote, Antonio, 125
Mitchell, Warren, 89
Mullen, Barbara, 183, 184
Murby, Leslie, 127
Murphy, Richard, 17, 30, 31, 37

New York, arrival in, 13–14
The New Yorker, 30
Newton, Robert, 108
Nicholas, Clive, 127–28
Noble, Bertie and Bill, 114–15

O'Brien, Catherine, 93, 120
Oeser, Oscar, 4, 119
O'Hara, Gerry, 100
O'Hara, John, 31
Olembert, Theodora, 136–40
Ostrer brothers, 67, 71

Pagnol, Marcel, xiii
Pictorial Research, Inc., 30, 39
Pilgrim Street, 86, 141
Pollard, Jack, 5–6
Preminger, Otto, 34, 65
Price, Dennis, 79

Quartet, 69, 72, 74, 78
Quayle, Anthony, 146

Radford, Basil, 98
Ramsdell, Joey, 111, 113

Rank, J. Arthur, 8, 68, 97. *See also* J. Arthur Rank Organisation
Rank Organisation. *See* J. Arthur Rank Organisation
Read, Professor John, F. R. S., 2, 6, 102
Rebecca's Daughters, 80
Richards, Pennington, 136
Richards, Silvia, 59, 62, 63
Ridley, Arnold, 106
Robin Hood, 142–43
Rogers, Peter, 73
The Roman Spring of Mrs. Stone, 55, 113
Ross, Harold, 30
Rotha, Paul, 1, 5. *See also* Strand Film Company

Schneer, Charles, 132–35
Scott, Daphne, 86, 96
Scott, Sir Harold, 86
Screenwriters Club, 92
Secret beyond the Door. *See* Lang, Fritz
The Secret Tent, 123
Selvin, Min, 60, 62
semidocumentary, in the United States, 8, 16
The Seventh Veil, 70
Sheldon, Kevin, 142
Sherlock Holmes, 136
Silva Bermúdez, Natalia, 50–54, 119–20, 130
Simpson, Bill, 103, 104
Skouras, Spyros, 15–16
Smart, Ralph, 75, 80, 81, 94, 144
So Long at the Fair, 78
Spanish Cooking at Home and on Holiday, 128
Spanish Paradors, 129

Spoonhandle. *See* de Rochemont, Louis
St. Andrews: as a model for *Dr. Finlay's Casebook*, 101–2; prewar life in, 2–4, 6–7
St. John, Earl, 95–96, 115
St. Leonards School, film of, 4, 5
Station X, 119
Strand Film Company, 5–6
Strange Report, 146
Strickling, Howard, 37, 40
Sullivan, John, 95, 97, 99

television, early days of, 141
Tenser, Tony, 99–100
Terry, John, 138, 140
That Kind of Girl, 99–101
Thomas, Dylan: and *The Beach of Falesa*, 80, 81–82; and *Me and My Bike*, 83–84; as a person, 81; as a scriptwriter, 81; early films of, 79–80; financial difficulties of, 80
Thurber, James, 31
Todd, Norman, 108, 128
Triangle Films, 137–38
Trio, 69, 78
Tutin, Dorothy, 109

Universal Pictures, 59

van Dongen, Helen, 54
Veiller, Anthony, 116
Venice Film Festival, 138
Vetter, Chuck, 123, 124
Vosper, Margery, 73, 96, 136
Vyse, Charles, 110–12
Vyse, John, 102, 114

Wanger, Walter, 59, 63
Warner, Jack, 89, 90

wartime research, 7–8
Weinstein, Hannah, 143
Wellington Square, Chelsea, 105–6
White Corridors, 97–98
Williams, Cara, 23
Willis, Ted (later Lord), 74, 87, 88, 89, 90, 91

Winner, Michael, 135
Withers, Googie, 98
Wolff, Lothar, 127

You Must Be Joking, 135

Zanuck, Darryl, 37, 41–42, 65

About the Author

Jan Read was born in Australia and brought up and educated in Scotland. Upon receiving a Commonwealth Fund Fellowship for studying cinematography in the United States, he worked with Louis de Rochemont at 20th Century–Fox and Fritz Lang at Universal-International. Upon returning to England, he became scenario editor for the British producer Sydney Box, who gave Read his first opportunity to write a full-length script, which became the film *The Blue Lamp*.

After spending many years in the motion picture and television industries, he became interested in writing and has since authored a great number of books on wine, travel, and gastronomy. He is also a regular contributor to *Decanter* and other leading British, American, and Spanish wine magazines. He is former honorary secretary of the British Circle of Wine Writers and a member of various wine orders, as well as a founding member of the Gran Orden de Caballeros del Vino. He was recently awarded the Gold Medal of the Gastronomische Akademie Deutchlands for the German edition of *Guide to the Wines of Spain*.